TRAILS OF
THE NORTH DAKOTA
BADLANDS & PRAIRIE

HIRAM ROGERS

TRAILS OF
THE NORTH DAKOTA
BADLANDS & PRAIRIE

A GUIDE TO THE MAAH DAAH HEY TRAIL,
THEODORE ROOSEVELT NATIONAL PARK,
& DAKOTA PRAIRIE GRASSLANDS

trails books

AN IMPRINT OF BOWER HOUSE

DENVER

Designed by Margaret McCullough
Maps by Rebecca Finkel
Photography by Hiram Rogers and Jean Gauger, and also thanks to Shutterstock.com

Printed in Canada

Library of Congress Control Number: 2020935161
ISBN 978-1-934553-79-4

10 9 8 7 6 5 4 3 2 1

Disclaimer: Risk is always a factor in backcountry and cave travel. Many of the activities described in this book can be dangerous, especially when weather is adverse or unpredictable, and when unforeseen events or conditions create a hazardous situation. The author has done his best to provide the reader with accurate information about backcountry travel as of the writing of this book, as well as to point out some of its potential hazards. It is the responsibility of the users of this guide to learn the necessary skills for safe travel, and to exercise caution in potentially hazardous areas, especially on steep and difficult terrain. The author and publisher disclaim any liability for injury or other damage caused by backcountry traveling, or performing any other activity described in this book.

TABLE OF CONTENTS

Acknowledgments x

INTRODUCTION 1
Using this Guide 3
Enjoying the Outdoors 10
Recommended Trips 12

1 THEODORE ROOSEVELT NATIONAL PARK 15
Entry Fees and Visitor Centers 17
Camping and Picnic Areas 17
Hiking 19
Biking 21
Horseback Riding 21
Backcountry Camping 22
Painted Canyon Trail, South Unit 25
Lone Tree Loop Trail, South Unit 29
Jones Creek – Lower Paddock Creek Trails Loop 33
Roundup Trail, South Unit 37
Upper Paddock Creek –
    Upper Talkington Trails Loop, South Unit 39
Old East Entrance Station Trail, South Unit 43
Petrified Forest Trails Loop, South Unit 47
Caprock Coulee Trail, North Unit 53
Buckhorn Trail, North Unit 57
Achenbach Trails Loop, North Unit 61

Other Theodore Roosevelt National Park Trails 65
Painted Canyon Nature Trail 65
Skyline Vista Trail 65
Ridgeline Nature Trail 65
Coal Vein Nature Trail 65
Buck Hill Trail 66
Boicourt Overlook Trail 66
Wind Canyon Nature Trail 66
CCC Trail 66
Mike Auney Trail 67
Jones Creek Trail 67
Maah Daah Hey Trail 67
Medora Bike Path 68
Little Mo Nature Trail 68

Other Adventures in
Theodore Roosevelt National Park 69
Canoeing the Little Missouri River 69
The Park's Scenic Drives 71
Elkhorn Ranch Unit 73

2 MAAH DAAH HEY NATIONAL RECREATION TRAIL 75
Burning Coal Vein Campground to Toms Wash Trailhead .. 89
Toms Wash Trailhead to Plumely Draw Trailhead 93
Plumely Draw Trailhead to Sully Creek Campground 97
Sully Creek Campground to Wannagan Campground 101
Wannagan Campground to Elkhorn Campground 107
Elkhorn Campground to Magpie Campground 111
Magpie Campground to Bennett Trail 117
Bennett Trail to CCC Campground 123

3 LITTLE MISSOURI NATIONAL GRASSLAND 129
Buffalo Gap Trail 133
Ice Caves Trail 137
Cottonwood – Bennett – Maah Daah Hey Trails Loop 141
Long X – Maah Daah Hey Trails Loop 145

Other Little Missouri National Grassland Trails 149
Juniper Spur Trail 149
Maah Daah Hey Connecting Trails 149
Buffalo Gap Campground Trails 149
Aspen Trail and Hanson Overlook Trail 150
Summit and Summit View Trails 150
Sunset Trail 151
Wolf Trail 151

4 North Country National Scenic Trail &
The Sheyenne National Grassland 153
North Country National Scenic Trail, Southwest Section .. 157
North Country National Scenic Trail,
    Iron Springs Creek Section 161
Oak Leaf Trail Loop 165

Other Sheyenne National Grassland Trails
& North Country Trail 169
North Country Trail, Sheyenne National Grassland 169
Hankinson Hills Trail, Sheyenne National Grassland 169
Fort Ransom State Park Section,
    North Country National Scenic Trail 170
Lake Sakakawea State Park Section,
    North Country National Scenic Trail 171

5 OTHER NORTH DAKOTA AREAS 173
White Butte Route, Highest Point in North Dakota 173
Indian-Travois Trails Loop,
    Little Missouri State Park 177
Village Trail, Knife River Indian Villages Historic Site   181
North Forest Trail, Knife River
    Indian Villages National Historic Site 185

Other Trails 188
Cross Ranch State Park and Nature Preserve 188
Fort Union Trading Post National Historic Site 189

REFERENCES
Appendix A Selected Bibliography 190
Appendix B Information Sources 191
Additional Services: Medora and Watford City 192
Author Biography 194

TABLES
Table 1 Trip Planner 4
Table 2 Waterboxes 83
Table 3 Maah Daah Hey Trail Mileage 85

MAPS
Map A North Dakota Location Map ix
Map B Theodore Roosevelt National Park South-Unit 24
Map C Theodore Roosevelt National Park North-Unit 52
Map D-1 Maah Daah Hey Trail System North 74
Map D-2 Maah Daah Hey Trail System South 76
Map E Sheyenne National Grasslands 156
Map F White Butte 172
Map G Little Missouri State Park 176
Map H Knife River Indian Villages National Historic Site ... 180

Purple clouds over Theodore Roosevelt National Park

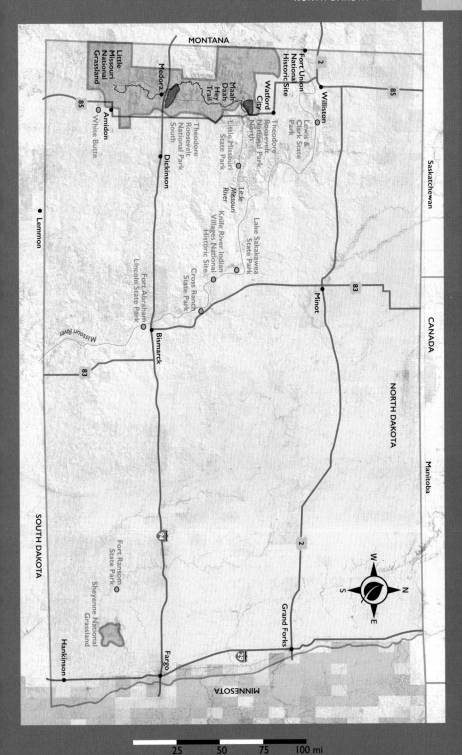

MONTANA

Little Missouri National Grassland

Fort Union National Historic Site

Williston

Medora

Maah Daah Hey Trail

Watford City

Lewis & Clark State Park

Theodore Roosevelt National Park North

85

Amidon

White Butte

Theodore Roosevelt National Park South

Little Missouri State Park

Little Missouri River

Dickinson

Lake Sakakawea State Park

Knife River Indian Villages National Historic Site

Lemmon

Cross Ranch State Park

Minot

83

Fort Abraham Lincoln State Park

Missouri River

Bismarck

83

Saskatchewan

CANADA

Manitoba

NORTH DAKOTA

Fort Ransom State Park

Sheyenne National Grassland

SOUTH DAKOTA

94

2

Grand Forks

Hankinson

Fargo

29

MINNESOTA

N W S E

25   50   75   100 mi

X

ACKNOWLEDGMENTS

This guide would not have been possible without the able assistance of many people. For the first edition of this guide, I am immensely grateful for help from Curt Glasoe, formerly of the Dakota Prairie Grasslands; Bruce Kaye, Theodore Roosevelt National Park; Jane Muggli, Theodore Roosevelt Nature and History Association; Terrence O'Halloran, Knife River Indian Villages National Historic Site; Phil Sjursen, Dakota Prairie Grasslands; and Russ Walsh, Dakota Prairie Grasslands.

For this new second edition, I'd like to thank Curt Glasoe of the Maah Daah Hey Trail Association, Russ Walsh and Will Horneman of the Dakota Prairie Grasslands, and Grant Geis of Theodore Roosevelt National Park for their reviews and assistance.

My wife, Jean, shares my fondness for this remarkable area. She read much of the manuscript, scouted many of the trails with me, provided some badly needed car shuttles, and endured many evenings filled with my muttering, scrawling, and thrashing through trail maps. Without her love, humor, and patience, this project would never have been completed.

INTRODUCTION

The badlands of western North Dakota are a beautiful and unique area. The exceptional potential of this wonderful recreation area has only recently been developed and is still being discovered by hikers, mountain bikers, and horseback riders. This guidebook focuses on hiking, mountain biking, and horseback trips in two main areas: Theodore Roosevelt National Park (TRNP) and the surrounding Dakota Prairie Grasslands (DPG), including the 144-mile long Maah Daah Hey (MDH) National Recreation Trail. The guide also covers some of the North Country National Scenic Trail in the Sheyenne National Grassland in the eastern part of the state, trails at Knife River Indian Villages National Historic Site in central North Dakota, plus some other related trails.

Theodore Roosevelt National Park has three units. There are trails in the North and South units which are about 50 miles apart, but none in the Elkhorn Ranch Unit which lies midway between the other two. The Dakota Prairie Grasslands manages the Little Missouri (LMNG), Sheyenne (SNG), and Grand River (GRNG) National Grasslands. The Maah Daah Hey trail system is in the LMNG, while the North Country and related trails are in the SNG.

Some of the material in this book first appeared in *Exploring the Black Hills and Badlands: A Guide for Hikers, Cross-country Skiers, and Mountain Bikers*. When that guidebook was first published in 1993, the only significant trail systems in western North Dakota were

LEFT Rugged badlands near Summit Trail.
ABOVE Rabbitbrush can be eaten by pronghorn or deer.

in Theodore Roosevelt National Park, so it made sense to cover North Dakota in a single chapter of a larger book. The completion of the original 96 miles of the Maah Daah Hey Trail led to the publication of the first edition of this guide in 2006. That book was the first and only detailed guide to the Maah Daah Hey Trail. By 2006, the Maah Daah Hey Trail was established as a tremendous success with mountain bikers, horseback riders, and hikers, and had spawned a second wave of trail building in the Dakota Prairie Grasslands. Between Theodore Roosevelt National Park, Dakota Prairie Grasslands, and state parks there were 300 miles of trails in western North Dakota, plus there were nearly another 100 miles of trails in the Sheyenne and Grand River districts of the DPG, the Knife River Indian Villages National Historic Site, and various North Dakota state parks. But with the completion of several new trails, there are now 450 miles of trail in the areas covered by this guide.

After several years of the first edition being out of print, demand for information about the Maah Daah Hey Trail and the North Dakota badlands has resulted in a new edition of this guide. The driving change for this second edition was the completion of the new 47-mile southern portion of the Maah Daah Hey Trail from the Sully Creek State Park Campground south to the Little Missouri National Grassland's Burning Coal Vein Campground. This addition extends the Maah Daah Hey to 144 miles, making it the longest single-track trail in the region.

Since the release of the first edition, the Dakota Prairie Grasslands has also completed the Wolf Trail, between Watford City and the North Unit of Theodore Roosevelt National Park, as well as the Oak Leaf Trail, which forms a loop with east end of the North Country Trail in the Sheyenne National Grassland. In Theodore Roosevelt National Park, the East Entrance Trail in the South Unit has been added to the trail system. TRNP has also revised the names of many of their trails so that most major trail segments now have unique names. At White Butte, due to landowner concerns, the old east side route is now off limits and there is a new designated access route on the north side.

The release of the second edition also provided the opportunity to include more detailed trail descriptions. In TRNP, I've added expanded coverage of the Painted Canyon Trail, Roundup Trail, and Lone Tree Loop Trail. In the LMNG the descriptions of the Ice Caves, Cottonwood-Bennett-MDH loop, and Long X-MDH loop have been extended. In the SNG chapter, I've added details on the southwest section of the North Country Trail and the Iron Springs section of the NCT. I've also added more information on the Village and North Forest Trails at the Knife River Indian Villages National Historic Site.

The success and popularity of the Maah Daah Hey Trail has led to the development of a series of side trails in the surrounding grasslands which add numerous opportunities for day trips and loop hikes. The first and most important of these is the Buffalo Gap Trail, which was built to offer mountain bikers a route around the wilderness area in the South Unit of Theodore Roosevelt National Park. The Dakota Prairie Grasslands has used the Maah Daah Hey Trail as the backbone of a system of trails unparalleled in the National Grasslands system. Fourteen other trails form short loops and link the Maah Daah Hey Trail to various campgrounds and to the Ice Caves.

The extensive trail system at Little Missouri State Park to the northeast of TRNP and the LMNG is included again in this update. This trail system has grown to 48 miles since my first visit in 1992. The park has become very popular with horseback riders, but is sadly overlooked by hikers who are missing out on some outstanding badlands scenery.

One of the difficulties of writing trail guides is anticipating changes that might take place while the guide is in print. Hopefully new trails will continue to be added to the systems in the national parks, national grasslands, and state park systems. Maintenance activities are ongoing at all these areas, and sometimes will require significant reroutes. Other times trail names may change, listed mileages may vary, or allowed uses can change. It is always a good policy to check with the land manager for the latest updates and trail conditions.

USING THIS GUIDE

The trips described in this guide range from short, self-guided interpretive trails, such as Caprock Coulee Nature Trail in Theodore Roosevelt National Park, to multiday expeditions, such as a trip along the entire Maah Daah Hey Trail. While each trip may not be suitable for everyone, there is a broad range of trip ideas ranging from outings for families with children to suggestions for experienced backpackers looking for multiday excitement. Trips are included for hikers, mountain bike riders, and horseback riders. Table 1 summarizes the trips, their length, difficulty, and allowed uses.

The book is divided into five main sections. The first covers the trails in Theodore Roosevelt National Park. The next two cover the Maah Daah Hey Trail and the rest of the trails on the Little Missouri National Grassland. The fourth section includes the North Country National Scenic Trail, and other trails in the Sheyenne National Grassland. The final section covers other trails outside of areas listed above, including White Butte, Little Missouri State Park, and Knife River Indian Villages National Historic Site.

TABLE 1 - TRIP PLANNER

AREA	TRAIL NAME	DIST	RATING	FAMILY	MB	HORSE	BP
TRNP-S	Painted Canyon Trail	4.2	M	Y	N	Y	N
TRNP-S	Lone Tree Loop Trail	9.3	D	P	N	Y	Y
TRNP-S	Jones Creek-Lower Paddock Creek Trails Loop	11.4	M	P	N	Y	Y
TRNP-S	Roundup Trail	6.6	M	Y	N	Y	N
TRNP-S	Upper Talkington/Upper Paddock Creek Trails	16.4	D	N	N	Y	Y
TRNP-S	Old East Entrance Station	1.0	E	Y	N	N	N
TRNP-S	Petrified Forest Loop	10.4	M	P	N	Y	Y
TRNP-N	Caprock Coulee Nature Trail	4.1	M	Y	N	N	N
TRNP-N	Buckhorn Trail	11.4	MD	N	N	Y	Y
TRNP-N	Achenbach Trail Loop	19.3	D	N	N	Y	Y

TABLE 1 - TRIP PLANNER

AREA	TRAIL NAME	DIST	RATING	FAMILY	MB	HORSE	BP
MDH	Burning Coal Vein CG to Toms Wash TH	15.5	M	N	Y	Y	Y
MDH	Toms Wash TH to Plumely Draw TH	17.8	M	N	Y	Y	Y
MDH	Plumely Draw TH to Sully Creek Campground	13.9	M	P	Y	Y	Y
MDH	Sully Creek Campground to Wannagan Campground	17.6	M	P	P	Y	Y
MDH	Wannagan Campground to Elkhorn Campground	20.8	M	N	Y	Y	Y
MDH	Elkhorn Campground to Magpie Campground	19.7	D	N	Y	Y	Y
MDH	Magpie Campground to Bennett Trail	22.1	M	N	Y	Y	Y
MDH	Bennett Trail to CCC Campground	16.9	M	N	P	Y	Y
LMNG	Buffalo Gap Trail	19.0	M	N	Y	Y	Y
LMNG	Ice Caves Trail	3.0	E	Y	Y	Y	N

TABLE 1 - TRIP PLANNER

AREA	TRAIL NAME	DIST	RATING	FAMILY	MB	HORSE	BP
LMNG	Cottonwood - Bennett - MDH Trails Loop	15.1	M	N	Y	Y	Y
LMNG	Long X - MDH Trails Loop	11.3	M	N	Y	Y	N
DPG	North Country National Scenic Trail, Southwest Section	12.2	M	N	Y	Y	Y
DPG	North Country National Scenic Trail - Iron Springs Creek Section	8.4	M	Y	Y	Y	Y
DPG	Oak Leaf Loop	4.2	E	Y	Y	Y	N
ND	White Butte Route, Highest Point in North Dakota	3.5	E	Y	N	N	N
ND	Indian-Travois Trails Loop, Little Missouri State Park	5.3	M	Y	N	Y	N
ND	Villages Trail, Knife River Indian Villages National Historic Site	1.7	E	Y	N	N	N
ND	North Forest Trail, Knife River Indian Villages National Historic Site	4.9	E	Y	N	N	N

The first three chapters begin with an overview of the natural and cultural history of that area. General background information on the features of the area follows, along with a summary of that area's rules and regulations. Next come the trip descriptions, which are given in two levels of detail. The most popular, or most deserving, trips are described in detail, while some of the other trails and routes are briefly described. Those described as "trails" follow officially mapped and maintained trails. Those described as routes (White Butte and any suggestions for off-trail travel) follow unmaintained and unsigned routes of my own creation. Trails will appeal to all experience levels, but routes are best left to more experienced people.

Each detailed trip profile begins with a brief description that also indicates which user groups are allowed and how difficult the trip is. This heading, along with the information in Table 1, is designed to help visitors quickly select the trip that is right for them. The allowed uses of a trail vary according to the land management agency. Most importantly for users of this guide, note that mountain bikes are not allowed on the trails in Theodore Roosevelt National Park or in Knife River Indian Villages National Historic Site.

Trail difficulty can be very tough to gauge. Distance, elevation changes, and roughness of footing are the most important factors. But the weather on any particular day can make a bike trail slippery or leave a hiker cold and wet. Since there is such a range between the strongest hikers seeking challenging trips and casual hikers seeking shorter diversions, these ratings can only be a rough estimate. When planning your trip, keep in mind both the rating and distance. The terrain on a twenty-mile stretch of flat trail may be easy, but it doesn't take long for all those miles to add up. If you're not sure of your abilities, be conservative. The longer trips will always be there to challenge you on later visits. I can tell you from hard-earned experience that it is better to have some energy left when you get back to the car than to struggle through a long afternoon simply hoping to reach the end of the trail.

"General Location" lets you easily find a trail from the nearest town using either a highway map or your favorite mapping software.

"Trip Highlights" helps readers select trails that will most interest them. Here you'll find out if a particular trail is known for wildlife watching, has outstanding vistas, or is ideal for seekers of solitude.

"Access" gives detailed turn-by-turn driving directions on how to reach each trailhead from a nearby town or major highway. GPS waypoints are given for trailheads and important landmarks. For one-way trips, directions to both trailheads are given. In much of the area road names can be confusing as federal and local agencies use different systems for road names. I've attempted to use the county and Dakota Prairie Grasslands road names (DPG 711, for example) as much as possible in my trailhead access descriptions as these are most likely to appear on published maps. However, I've also included local road names (140 Street SW, for example) which are more likely to appear on signs outside of the DPG.

"Distance" is given in miles for each trip and often for optional variations. These distances may vary somewhat from those listed elsewhere. In a few cases distances have been measured more accurately, and in others I've chosen a slightly different version of a popular trip. My own trail measurements have been with either a bike odometer or a handheld GPS unit.

"Allowed Uses" summarizes whether mountain bikes, horses, or overnight trips are allowed.

Finally, there is a list of useful trail maps. The maps contained in this guide are based on the official maps from the parks and grasslands units described here. A few changes have been made as a result of my own experiences in the field. Most of the areas described in the first three chapters of this guide are covered by the National Geographic Trails Illustrated map of Theodore Roosevelt National Park, which also covers all of the current Maah Daah Hey Trail system. Rather than try to replicate all the mapping information in the Trails Illustrated map, this guide presents generalized trail maps and refers those wanting more detail and a topographic base to the Trails Illustrated map.

ABOVE Trails in Theodore Roosevelt NP and the Dakota Prairie Grassland are well-signed.

Those looking for the latest Maah Daah Hey Trail maps have two resources. The Maah Daah Hey Trail Association website has a superb online interactive map and has GPX file downloads for the Maah Daah Hey and its associated trails. The 2018 version of the LMNG Maah Daah Hey National Recreation Trail map is currently the most up-to-date print resource.

Two other sets of maps will also prove useful to the outdoors lover. The 1974 U.S. Geological Survey (USGS) maps for both the South and North units of Theodore Roosevelt National Park are still available online from the USGS at a scale more detailed than the Trails Illustrated map. The 7.5-minute USGS 1:24,000 quadrangles for western North Dakota were recently updated and now show the Maah Daah Hey Trail. The relevant USGS maps along with any other important park maps are listed. Keep in mind that the USGS quadrangles sometimes show an older route of the Maah Daah Hey Trail that was changed since publication of the USGS topo maps.

The level of detail contained in trip descriptions corresponds to the difficulty of finding your way. Descriptions for well-marked trails are brief, while those for obscure trails or unmaintained routes are very detailed. It is a good idea to check with the appropriate management agency (see Appendix B) before starting on an unfamiliar trail, and to check your map each time you stop when on an unfamiliar trail or route. To help mountain bikers in selecting their trips, the surface for each trip is described as a trail, two-track dirt road, maintained dirt road, or gravel road.

Global positioning system (GPS) units have become popular instruments for both techies and outdoors lovers. GPS units use readings from a satellite network to triangulate the position of the unit, often to within 50 feet. I've used a GPS to map most of the trails in this guide and have included GPS waypoints for all trailheads, trail intersections, and other key points along the way. The Trails Illustrated map has both latitude and longitude and UTM coordinates using an NAD 27 Datum. If you depend on GPS for your navigation, remember that it sometimes can be impossible to get GPS readings, especially in canyon bottoms, and that a good, old-fashioned map and compass sometimes may still be needed for navigation.

The road network in the Dakota Prairie Grasslands is constantly evolving, especially as long as the current oilfield boom continues. There may be more roads than are shown on U.S. Geological Survey, Trails Illustrated, or DPG maps. Avoid the temptation to navigate solely by watching road intersections. I have simplified the DPG road classification system by calling all roads by number with a DPG prefix, regardless of which grassland they may be in. These roads generally are permanent, signed, and have numbers, such as DPG Road 808. These roads may also have county road numbers and names.

Trail systems throughout the region are being expanded and improved. Be aware that a trail guide cannot remain current forever and that the conditions of trail markers can deteriorate over time. If you find an error in a trail description or other notable feature, or discover a relocation in one of the trails, let us know about it so we can include the change in the next edition of this book. Write me in care of the publisher at: Bower House, PO Box 7459, Denver, CO 80207. For more information on the publisher, visit www.bowerhousebooks.com.

ENJOYING THE OUTDOORS

Most trails described in this guide can be used nearly year-round for hiking, mountain biking, and horseback riding. Though winter usually is too severe to enjoy outdoor recreation, a few days may be warm and calm enough to enjoy some sheltered hiking. A few trails described here are also groomed for cross-country skiing. Cool temperatures, without lingering snow, can make spring hiking ideal. In summer, escape from the heat by mountain biking, hiking in the woods along a cool river, or by leaving the work to a willing horse. In fall, dry soil and mild weather combine to allow superb hiking and riding anywhere in the region.

DAY HIKES in western North Dakota require only a little advance planning before you set out. You need to know the length of the route and whether the trip requires a car shuttle. In summer, your main worries are drinking water and protection from the sun and wind. Essential items to carry include food, water, a first aid kit, sunscreen, lip balm, and a hat for shade, along with a map and this guide. Few trailheads provide drinking water, and you should never drink untreated water. Snakes, bison, and other wildlife can pose hazards for hikers. Do not disturb any wildlife you encounter. Be aware that poison ivy grows in many moist areas and don't forget to do a tick check at the end of your hike.

BACKPACKING skills for the North Dakota badlands can be quite different from those used in other areas. Badlands backpackers are exposed to an all-day onslaught of sun and wind. The major factor in trip planning is that some areas have no water, so you must bring what you need with you. The weight and bulk of a large water supply can be a major burden on a long trip, so some parties in Theodore Roosevelt National Park may elect to hike in a short distance and set up a base camp. Another alternative, especially for those hiking long distances on the Maah Daah Hey Trail, is to cache water along your route in the trail's waterboxes, or plan to stay at the Maah Daah Hey campgrounds. Badlands backpackers don't suffer the physical toil of hauling heavy loads up high mountains, but they are exposed to extremes of weather in an unforgiving wilderness terrain. However, the views here are always 360 degrees, nature's bounty is readily apparent, and many of these areas are true wilderness seen by few other visitors.

MOUNTAIN BIKING The Dakota Prairie Grasslands are paradise for mountain bike riders. The Maah Daah Hey and the other trails around it are scenic, challenging, and relatively uncrowded. The new sections of the Maah Daah Hey Trail south of Sully Creek State Park are especially attractive both because of their bike-friendly design and the easy access to major roads. Mountain bikers should also prepare for their trips with an eye on the weather. A gentle rain, or even a heavy dew, can turn a normally easy trail into an unridable obstacle course of sticky, slippery gumbo. A good rule of thumb is that if you are making a distinct tire mark in the trail, that trail is too wet to ride. Be sure to bring repair tools, a tire pump, and patch kits. Don't plan on being able to call for a ride if things go wrong, there is little cellphone reception along the trail. Riders should also wear a helmet and gloves for those inevitable crashes.

HORSEBACK RIDING is another popular activity on the Maah Daah Hey Trail and on the trails in Theodore Roosevelt National Park. Riders should keep in mind that conditions in both the national park and national grasslands are primitive. Water, potable or not, is difficult to find away from the major rivers. Trails can be extremely slick when wet or even just damp. Riding on wet trails can severely erode them, so confine your trips to dry conditions. There is no longer a horse riding concession at the South Unit of Theodore Roosevelt National Park. All riding areas described here require certified weed-free feed for horses.

FAMILY TRIPS are listed in Table 1. These trips are short and easy enough to accommodate younger hikers and have the high-impact features and end-of-trail rewards that will hold the interest of youngsters. If a trail is too long for families, but a shorter piece is suitable, it is marked with a "P" for partial in Table 1.

All-terrain vehicle (ATV) use is becoming more widespread. The Forest Service nationwide has identified unregulated off-road vehicle use as one of the most significant threats facing our national forests. All of the National Park, many parts of the Dakota Prairie Grasslands, and most of

the trails described here are closed to vehicle use. The Forest Service
has completed a major shift in the way that it manages transportation so
that ATV use is permitted only where specifically designated.

RECOMMENDED TRIPS

The trips listed below generally are my personal favorites, although
some were chosen with the help of other experts. Most have at least
one or two special features such as tremendous views, wilderness
solitude, or wildlife watching to recommend them. If you don't
have a lot of time to explore the area, these are the trips to take.

BEST SHORT FAMILY HIKES
- Painted Canyon Trail, TRNP South Unit
- Lower Paddock Creek Trail to the prairie dog towns,
  TRNP South Unit
- Old East Entrance Station, TRNP South Unit
- Caprock Coulee Nature Trail, TRNP, North Unit
- Maah Daah Hey Trail, Sully Creek State Park
  south to Little Missouri River Overlook
- Oak Leaf Trail Loop, Sheyenne National Grassland
- White Butte Route, Highest Point in North Dakota
- Village Trail, Knife River Indian Village National Historic Site

BEST DAY HIKES
- Jones Creek – Lower Paddock Creek Loop, TRNP South Unit
- Upper Paddock Creek – Upper Talkington Loop,
  TRNP South Unit
- Petrified Forest Loop, TRNP South Unit
- Lone Tree Loop Trail, TRNP South Unit
- Buckhorn Trail north side, TRNP, North Unit
- Long X – Maah Daah Hey Loop, Little Missouri
  National Grassland
- Travois – Indian Trails Loop, Little Missouri State Park

BEST BACKPACK TRIPS
- Petrified Forest and Lone Tree Loop, TRNP South Unit
- Achenbach Loop, TRNP North Unit
- Wannagan Campground to the Little Missouri River,
  Maah Daah Hey Trail
- CCC Campground to the Little Missouri River,
  Maah Daah Hey Trail

BEST MOUNTAIN BIKE RIDES

- Burning Coal Vein Campground to Toms Wash Trailhead, Maah Daah Hey Trail
- Plumley Trailhead to Sully Creek Campground, Maah Daah Hey Trail
- Cottonwood and Bennett Trails Loop, Little Missouri National Grassland
- Buffalo Gap Trail, Little Missouri National Grassland
- Southwest Section, North Country National Scenic Trail, Sheyenne National Grassland

BEST ROAD BIKE RIDES

- South Unit Scenic Loop Drive
- North Unit Scenic Drive

ABOVE Bison grazing along the Painted Canyon Trail.

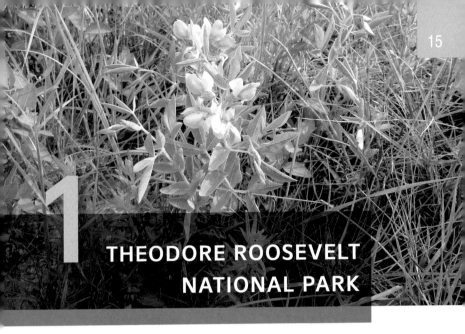

THEODORE ROOSEVELT NATIONAL PARK

Theodore Roosevelt is the national park that best exemplifies the spirit of the American West. Here one can imagine this rugged country as it was in the late 1800s, during the days of Roosevelt's cattle ranching. The landscape remains almost unchanged: humankind's influence on this unforgiving land has been modest. Just as during Roosevelt's tenure, only a few isolated ranches dot the landscape, and cattle ranching remains the primary occupation. The Little Missouri badlands may now be even richer in wildlife than they were then. Roosevelt arrived near the peak of the cattle boom when bison and other game species had been overhunted. Between the natural recovery of some populations and the reintroduction of others, the region's wildlife may now be even more prolific.

Theodore Roosevelt first came to the Dakotas in 1883 when western North Dakota was becoming known for its ranching and hunting opportunities. Even though few bison remained when Roosevelt first arrived for a hunt, he fell in love with the country and soon returned to try ranching. This was the era of open range, when cattle grazed without fences. Unfortunately for ranchers, this cattle boom was short lived. The harsh winter of 1886-1887 killed large numbers of stock, and the subsequent summers were much drier.

This short period in the Dakotas profoundly influenced Theodore Roosevelt. His Maltese Cross Ranch was located south of Medora, but he preferred life on his more isolated Elkhorn Ranch to the north. Ranching fit well with his philosophy of a vigorous life. His writings

LEFT A badlands butte in Painted Canyon.
ABOVE Goldenpea shows off its bright yellow flowers.

are filled with an appreciation for the quiet simplicity of ranch life and for the beauty of the natural world. He witnessed the near extinction of bison and emerged from the experience as a powerful force in American conservation. The beauty and solitude found today in this national park is a fitting tribute to the president who most strongly shaped our conservation ethic and our national park system.

The movement to establish a national park to honor the former president began soon after Roosevelt's death in 1917. The area was first designated a national wildlife refuge in 1946 and then it became a national memorial park in 1947. As the management focus of the area shifted from historic preservation to broader stewardship of natural resources, the area was designated Theodore Roosevelt National Park in 1978.

Theodore Roosevelt National Park is divided into three separate units separated by 40 miles of private land and Dakota Prairie Grasslands. The South Unit, located adjacent to Interstate 94 (I-94) near Medora, covers 46,000 acres and receives the most visitors. Forty miles

ABOVE Wild horses are a primary attraction for visitors to Theodore Roosevelt NP.

north, off US 85 near Watford City, the North Unit covers 24,000 acres. Between the two units, set snuggly against the Little Missouri River is the 218-acre Elkhorn Ranch Unit, nearly as isolated now as when Roosevelt lived there. The three areas are tied together by the region's lifeline, the waters of the Little Missouri River.

In addition to protection as a national park, three parcels also were designated as the Theodore Roosevelt Wilderness in 1978. In the South Unit, 10,500 acres—including most of the area west of the Little Missouri—is designated wilderness. In the North Unit, 19,400 acres—in two areas split by the Scenic Drive—are also designated wilderness. Wilderness designation gives these lands the highest degree of protection possible by prohibiting activities such as use of mechanized vehicles (including mountain bikes) or the building of roads or other permanent structures.

ENTRY FEES AND VISITOR CENTERS

A seven-day entry pass to the park cost $30 per vehicle in 2019. A variety of other passes are available through the National Park Service. Most visitors will first stop by one of the park's three visitor centers. The park is open 24 hours per day year-round, however most facilities are closed on major holidays and have reduced hours outside of the summer season. For the latest information check the park website at www.nps.gov/thro.

The South Unit Visitor Center is in the town of Medora just off Interstate 94 at exits 24 or 27 and is open 8:00 a.m. to 6:00 p.m. Mountain Time in summer. Tours of Roosevelt's restored and relocated Maltese Cross cabin are conducted daily in summer.

The Painted Canyon Visitor Center is at Exit 32 on I-94, just east of Medora. It is open from 8:30 a.m. to 5:30 p.m. (MST) in summer.

The North Unit Visitor Center is located off US 85 south of Watford City. It is open 9 a.m. to 5 p.m. (CST) during the summer. The rest of the year it is open as staffing permits.

CAMPING AND PICNIC AREAS

In the South Unit, the Cottonwood Campground, which lies 5.6 miles from Medora on the Scenic Loop Drive, is open year-round. The campground is popular and typically fills to capacity each afternoon, mid-May through mid-September. The north loop has larger pull-through sites, and the south loop has smaller sites. There are no utility hookups. Of the 76 sites, 12 are walk-in tent sites. Half the sites are by reservation at recreation.gov while all remaining sites are first come, first served. In 2019, sites were $14 per night. Reservations are accepted only for the group camp (6 to 20 people). The campground has flush toilets (in summer only) and a pay phone, but does not have showers or cell phone reception. There are no dump facilities for trailers at the campground; the nearest dump facilities are in Medora. A full list of rules and a map are available at the check-in station, online, and any visitor center. Livestock, including horses, are not allowed in the campground. Pets must be kept on leash, a commonsense rule in an area that may be visited by bison, wild turkey, and other wildlife. The campground is open year-round with only well water and latrines available in winter, at a winter rate of $7.

The Juniper Campground, located at mile 4.6 on the North Unit Scenic Drive, also is open year-round. There are 44 sites in two loops with nine walk-in sites. Campsites are available on a first come, first served basis. Juniper Campground may fill to capacity by late afternoon in summer and generally fills to capacity on holiday weekends. In 2019, sites were $14 per night. Reservations are accepted only for the group camp (6 to 60 people). The campground has flush toilets (in summer) and a pay phone, but does not have showers or cell phone reception. Juniper has dump facilities for trailers. A full list of rules and a map are available at the check-in station, online, and any visitor center. Livestock, including horses, are not allowed in the campground. Pets must be kept on a leash, a reasonable rule for an area where game trails across the Little Missouri River may bring bison into your camp. Juniper Campground also can serve as the trailhead for the Achenbach, Buckhorn, and Little Missouri (Little Mo) Nature trails. In winter there are latrines only, and the nearest water source is the North Unit Visitor Center.

The Roundup Horse Camp is in the South Unit about two miles north of the end of the Scenic Loop Drive. Roundup is the park's only camping facility in which horses are permitted. Occupancy is limited to one group at a time. Reservations for Roundup begin each season on the first business day in March at 8:00 a.m. (MST). Roundup can accommodate up to 20 people and 20 horses, or 30 people if camping without horses. The nightly rate is $40. Facilities include vault toilets, drinking water, a pavilion and picnic area, plus corrals, hitch rails, and water tanks. There are no showers and no cell phone reception. Certified weed-free horse feed is required, and horses must follow designated trails. A full list of rules and a map are available at the check-in station and any visitor center. Other information on horse boarding around the park can be obtained from the park's visitor centers.

A wide variety of commercial campgrounds are located in communities around the park. Picnic areas are located next to the Cottonwood and Juniper campgrounds, at the Painted Canyon Visitor Center, and in Medora.

HIKING

No permits are needed for day hiking trips in the park, although it is always wise to ask at a visitor center for the latest trail conditions. Park trailheads are well-marked and now all have signboards featuring maps and distances for the trails. Trails are marked with large wooden and shorter carsonite posts. In some parts of the park, trails can be tough to follow, especially if the posts have been knocked over by bison. Bison and other wildlife also create their own trails that can become more obvious than the park's official trails. Also, be aware that in the bottom lands along the Little Missouri River, sagebrush can grow high enough to obscure trail markers.

Since the release of the first edition of this guide, the park has clarified some trail names. For example, the former Petrified Forest Loop is now split into three trails, part of which is now a section of the Maah

ABOVE Hiker on the North Petrified Forest Trail.

Daah Hey Trail, and the rest is either part of the North or South Petrified Forest trails. The Rim Trail now connects the Upper Paddock Creek and Upper Talkington trails, and the Badlands Spur Trail now connects Lower Paddock Creek and Lower Talkington trails.

If you plan to cross the Little Missouri River, make sure you check river levels before beginning your trip. Ask a ranger at a visitor center for the latest conditions. Remember also that wet weather can make much of the backcountry impassable, especially areas where the soil contains a bentonite clay, locally called gumbo. This devilish substance is firm and chalky gray when dry. But when wet gumbo has the unique ability to be both sticky and slippery at the same time. It can be too slick to walk on safely, and at the same time it can cling in huge heavy masses to boots, bike tires, and horse hooves.

Remember that all plants, animals, fossils, and historic artifacts in the park are protected and must be left undisturbed for the enjoyment of other visitors. The abundance of petrified wood in the park makes small pieces a tempting target for souvenir hunters, but all fossils should be left in place. Be especially careful to give wildlife a wide berth, at least 25 yards or more. In general, if an animal reacts to your presence, you are too close. Bison in particular can be unpredictable; lone bulls can be especially grumpy. Rolling in dirt or raising their tails (this display can mean "charge" or "discharge") are signs of agitation and a good warning for hikers to move away. More than likely you'll encounter ticks, and both poison ivy and rattlesnakes are found in the park.

One of the unusual things hikers notice about the trails at Theodore Roosevelt are the huge wooden posts used to mark some trails. The park uses a mix of wood and fiberglass posts, but it is the tall wood posts that really stand out. These monsters are usually six inches square, and five feet high. They are buried deeply in the ground, but nonetheless are often toppled by the ever-present bison. The bison, which use the trails more than people do, have nothing against trail markers. But they do love to scratch on the posts, particularly those dotting the grasslands where nature has left them few natural options. Presumably, scratching is the most intense in the spring when winter coats need to be shed in advance of summer's blast of heat. But year-round you'll find tufts of brown fur clinging to slivers of the marking posts. The bison will even try to scratch on the less sturdy fiberglass posts, often snapping those off at ground level. How many posts mark your trail will depend on the balance between the longing of bison for good scratching posts and the perseverance of the park rangers in replacing them.

Trail maintenance in the park varies with the resources the park is allocated each year. Bison are efficient, if unintentional, trail builders.

If you have strayed off the park trail onto a game trail, retrace your path back to a marked trail. However, a good map and attention to it is enough to keep most hikers on course in the open terrain. Cross-country travel on foot is allowed anywhere in the park, and route finding for those with maps and map reading skills is straightforward.

Spring and fall are the best times to visit the Little Missouri badlands. The change in seasons moderates the temperature extremes characteristic of the northern plains. Many visitors will find the heat and absence of shade in midsummer uncomfortable. Try to do most of your activity in the early morning or late evening. Summer hikers should be careful to avoid lightening storms, which killed a trail user in 2019. As always, keep an eye on the weather. It never takes long to go from dusty to downpour.

BIKING

There are no trails open to mountain bikes in Theodore Roosevelt National Park. Bikes must stay on paved or dirt roads, a restriction that leaves the Scenic Drives as the only realistic biking options in either park unit. The South Unit Scenic Drive is a 35.7-mile round trip from Medora and the North Unit Scenic Drive is a 27.4-mile round trip. In 2019 the park closed part of the South Unit Scenic Loop Drive due to slumping activity. The south side of the loop road is closed from the mile 7 closure gate to the Badlands Overlook at mile 11.5. Due to the large extent and high estimated cost of repair, a timeline for reopening the road is not available.

The Scenic Drives do not have road shoulders in all places and riders will be sharing the road with large recreational vehicles. However, there are numerous mountain biking options in the surrounding Dakota Prairie Grasslands, including the Buffalo Gap Trail that provides a bypass route for the Maah Daah Hey Trail around the South Unit of the park. For information on mountain biking on the Maah Daah Hey Trail and its surrounding trail network, see the following chapters.

HORSEBACK RIDING

A trip on horseback through Theodore Roosevelt National Park gives the same view from the saddle that Roosevelt himself had during his tenure in North Dakota. Horses are allowed on all the backcountry trails. Horses are not allowed on the developed nature trails, on roads, in campgrounds, or in picnic areas. Two popular riding trails from the Roundup Horse Camp are the Mike Auney Trail that leads west across the Little Missouri River to the Petrified Forest Loop Trail, and the Roundup Trail that leads east to intersect the Jones Creek Trail.

Horse trailers can be parked at any trailhead with parking spaces large enough to accommodate trailers. In the South Unit, the best locations to park are Peaceful Valley Ranch and the Lower Jones Creek trailhead. In the North Unit, the best locations are the Cannonball Concretions Pullout and Oxbow Overlook. Trailer parking may sometimes be possible at other trailheads, but should not be relied upon as these tend to fill with other, smaller vehicles.

Guided trail rides are no longer offered within the park, but commercial outfitters can be found in Medora. Those looking to organize their own trip can board horses at the Roundup Horse Camp with a reservation, or at private areas outside the park (check at the visitor center for a current list). You should make arrangements for horse boarding before arriving at the park.

Horse groups spending the night in the backcountry are subject to the backcountry camping regulations discussed below. Horseback riders on day trips are also subject to the same rules as other park visitors. The park has an overnight limit of eight horses and eight riders per group. Remember that grazing in the park is prohibited, and certified weed-free feed is required for your horses. Be especially careful not to harass wildlife. The park prohibits horses from coming within 300 yards of bison.

BACKCOUNTRY CAMPING

Anyone staying overnight in the backcountry of TRNP must obtain a free backcountry camping permit from a visitor center. Though the permits are free, park entry fees still apply. After your trip, please check out at the visitor center or return your permit. There are no designated campsites or restrictions on the number of parties. Campsites must be at least one-quarter mile from roads or trailheads and at least 200 feet from water sources. Party size limits are ten people, or eight people plus eight horses.

Backpackers and horse parties are subject to the same guidelines as those on day trips. In addition, the park requires all campers to practice Leave No Trace camping techniques. A full list of regulations is printed on the park backcountry trail map. Some important regulations include a ban on open fires in the backcountry, a ban on pets, the need for hikers to yield right-of-way to horses, and the need to carry out all trash including toilet paper (burying trash is prohibited). Dispose of human waste in a cat hole that is at least 200 feet from any campsite or water source.

Depending on your route, locations along the Little Missouri River or close to flowing wells will offer the best campsites. Due to the lack of drinking water in the backcountry, you will need to plan where to camp in advance of your trip to have access to water and the ability to treat it. Occasionally it is possible to get water from larger side creeks such as Knutson Creek, but these creeks only flow during the wettest seasons or immediately after storms. Wells and springs found in the backcountry have non-potable water suitable for wildlife and livestock only.

ABOVE Pronghorn are common across western North Dakota.

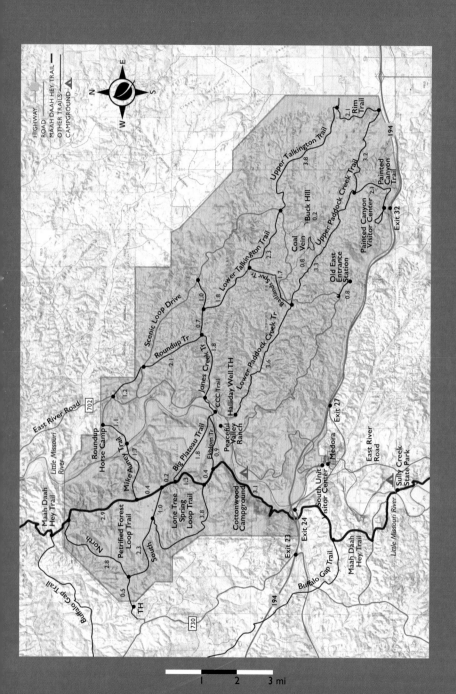

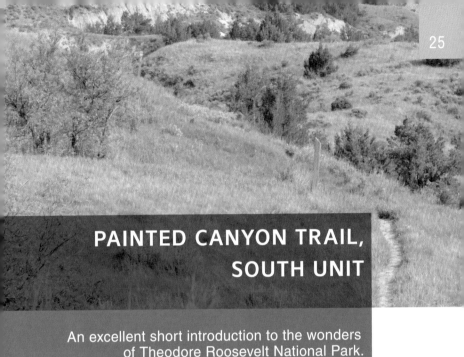

PAINTED CANYON TRAIL, SOUTH UNIT

An excellent short introduction to the wonders of Theodore Roosevelt National Park.

GENERAL LOCATION: Six miles east of Medora, North Dakota.

HIGHLIGHT: A short introduction to the park in one of its most scenic areas.

ACCESS: Exit 32 off Interstate 94 leads directly to parking at the Painted Canyon Visitor Center. The trailhead is at a prominent signboard at the east end of the parking area (N46 53.714, W103 22.798).

DISTANCE: This hike is 4.2 miles out and back.

ALLOWED USES: This trail is open to hikers and horseback riders.

MAPS: USGS Theodore Roosevelt National Park South Unit 1:24,000 special topographic map, Trails Illustrated Theodore Roosevelt National Park (#259), and Map B.

Many visitors to Theodore Roosevelt National Park receive their introduction to the park at Painted Canyon. Easy access directly off Interstate 94 ensures that in the busy summer travel season, the

ABOVE The view descending into Painted Canyon.

Painted Canyon Visitor Center will be crowded with families eager to experience the park's scenery and wildlife and ready to burn off pent-up energy from their long driving trip. Most visitors are content to browse the displays and merchandise inside the visitor center, and most will visit the interpretive displays and gape at the colorful scenery along the paved walkway at the canyon rim. Others will choose to walk the 1.1-mile Painted Canyon Nature Trail that begins at the west end of the picnic area. However, a lucky few have the time and energy for a deeper introduction to the park's vistas, flowers, and wildlife by walking the Painted Canyon Trail.

Before the creation of the national park, Painted Canyon operated as a commercial site from the 1930s to 1964. During the last 11 years, it was operated by the Noyes family. Painted Canyon is also the site of the park's web cam. The web cam is a great resource for current conditions in the park and is available through a link on the park's website.

The trail begins by following an old two-track service road east beside the rim of the canyon. At 0.2 mile, an unmarked path leads left to the rim. Though the unmarked path has been followed by many unsuspecting hikers, the left turn is not the correct trail. Continue east on the old road to a trail post at 0.4 mile at a trail post at a point where there is no further path east along the rim (N46 53.530, W103 22.205). Turn left and begin the short but steady descent north into the canyon. Sign in at the register box located a short way below the rim. The trail is marked by both wood and carsonite posts.

The descent reveals many of the secrets of the badlands topography. The tough sods of the overlying grasslands form the canyon rims. Once breeched, the soft rock layers below the grassland erode easily into steep slopes carved intricately by flowing water and the slumping of the weak rock and clay layers. Painted Canyon and the valley of Paddock Creek are excellent spots for observing wildlife. Give plenty of space (at least 25 yards) to any bison or elk you may encounter; if an animal reacts to your presence, you are too close.

Track your progress by watching the distinctive shapes of the buttes rising from the badlands. You'll descend through several rock layers containing petrified wood. At 1.7 miles, cross the main stem of Paddock Creek where a dry crossing is typically possible. Reach the signed junction with the Upper Paddock Creek Trail (N46 54.678, W103 22.511) at 2.1 miles. Upper Paddock Creek Trail leads right and east 3.2 miles to the junction with the Rim Trail; it also leads left and west 3.2 miles to the Scenic Loop Drive.

Return to the Painted Canyon Visitor Center by retracing your route. The return hike will allow you to enjoy views of the visitor center from below. Only the last 0.3 mile of the rim climb is steep trail.

ABOVE Prairie smoke with goldenpea.

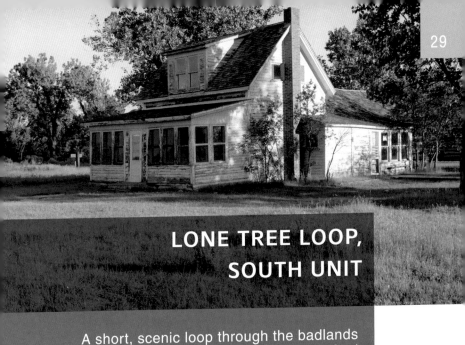

LONE TREE LOOP, SOUTH UNIT

A short, scenic loop through the badlands to Big Plateau that requires a ford of the Little Missouri River.

GENERAL LOCATION: Three miles north of Medora, North Dakota.

HIGHLIGHT: Badlands topography, diverse wildlife, and fossilized wood.

ACCESS: For the Peaceful Valley trailhead follow the Scenic Loop Road from the South Unit Visitor Center north for 6.6 miles to the start of the loop section. Stay left where the loop portion begins and turn left at 6.9 miles at the entrance to Peaceful Valley Ranch. The parking area, trailhead, and signboard are straight ahead in another 0.3 mile (N46 57.546, W103 30.259).

DISTANCE: The Lone Tree Loop is 9.3 miles around. A 5.4-mile loop can be made by connecting the Ekblom and Big Plateau trails via the Maah Daah Hey Trail rather than using the Lone Tree Loop Trail.

ALLOWED USES: This trail is open to hikers and horseback riders.

MAPS: USGS Theodore Roosevelt National Park South Unit 1:24,000 special topographic map, Trails Illustrated Theodore Roosevelt National Park (#259), and Map B.

LEFT Fall twilight in the badlands.
ABOVE Peaceful Valley Ranch serves as the trailhead for the Lone Tree Loop.

The Lone Tree Loop Trail is a wonderful introduction to the designated Wilderness Area on the west side of the South Unit. However, accessing this trail requires either a long approach hike via the Maah Daah Hey or Petrified Forest trails, or, more commonly, requires a ford of the Little Missouri River. Water levels in the Little Missouri are notoriously fickle. I've had to postpone several spring backpacking trips due to high water, but have often crossed easily by midsummer. Your best source for crossing information is the rangers at the South Unit Visitor Center in Medora. Check with them before you make any plans to ford the Little Mo. The river gauge at Medora can be found at https://waterdata.usgs.gov/nd/nwis/uv/?site_no=06336000&PARAmeter_cd=63158,00065,00060.

Since the horseback riding concession at Peaceful Valley closed in 2014, the ranch and trailhead have grown quieter, and now the most common visitors are hikers using the trailhead to cross the river.

From the trailhead, walk 0.2 mile to the east bank of the Little Missouri River (N46 57.638, W103 30.432). Ideally, you'll see a large sand and gravel bar on the near shore. Cross directly across the river from the upstream end of the bar. Generally, the river bottom here is

ABOVE The ford of the Little Missouri River near Peaceful Valley Ranch.

firm sand and gravel. Just beyond the crossing is an NPS register box. At 0.5 mile, reach the signed junction of the Ekblom and Big Plateau Trails (N46 57.730, W103 30.651) turn left to follow the Ekblom Trail and hike the loop clockwise.

The Ekblom Trail heads west up the flat sagebrush-filled valley of Knutson Creek. You'll soon enter a prairie dog town and then pass an old stock tank. You'll leave the dog town at the crossing of a small creek and reach the junction with the Maah Daah Hey Trail at 1.4 miles (N46 57.781, W103 31.766). The Knutson Creek valley beyond is wide, open, and scattered with small groves of trees which offer appealing backcountry camping options. At 1.8 miles, reach the split between the Lone Tree Loop and Maah Daah Hey trails (N46 57.925, W103 32.113) located just past the post for MDH MP 56 and cross Knutson Creek on a wooden bridge.

Turn right here to follow the Maah Daah Hey Trail if the shorter 5.4-mile loop is your goal for the day. The MDH will pass through a prairie dog town and then turn up the right side of a small draw. Pass MP 57 for the MDH at 2.8 miles, and then make a final climb past some petrified wood to reach the junction with the Big Plateau Trail at 3.1 miles, which is the 7.0-mile mark on the longer loop.

For the longer loop, bear left on the Lone Tree Loop Trail from the junction near Knutson Creek and continue to follow Knutson Creek upstream on its right side. The trail leaves the prairie dog town after another 0.5 mile, then passes a stock tank. At 4.1 miles, make an easy step-over crossing of Knutson Creek to the left side. The trail tread here is less distinct, but continue to follow the wood and carsonite trail posts. At 4.5 miles, two wood posts mark the junction with an old abandoned ranch track. The trail here has a deep backcountry feel. It is remote, scenic, and little used, exactly the way a wilderness should be.

The Lone Tree Loop Trail follows Knutson Creek to the northernmost point where the creek has enough flow to cut a channel (N46 59.066, W103 34.397). Ignore the game trails that continue upstream and turn right around the head of the ravine up a side draw with a long line of trees on the right. Lone Tree Spring is now hidden in the dense grove of trees at the head of this side draw. As you begin to climb to Big Plateau, cross a petrified wood location. The trail makes a final short steep climb before topping out on the plateau and reaching the junction with the South Petrified Forest Trail (N46 59.244, W103 33.370) at 5.8 miles.

Turn right to traverse a section of grasslands that appears to extend forever. A quick walk brings you to the "V" junction with the Maah Daah Hey Trail at 6.8 miles (N46 58.931, W103 32.265). Ignore the hard left turn onto the MDH which will lead you to the north, and instead continue straight ahead on the plateau top to follow the Maah Daah Hey south to the spilt with the Big Plateau Trail at 7.0 miles (N46 58.776, W103 32.162). Bear left at this split to follow the Big Plateau Trail down to another large prairie dog town which also attracts mule deer, coyotes, and bison. The trail crosses a distinct geologic horizon which contains many of the fossil trees that give name to the upper plateau. Several weathered fossil stumps are visible from the trail. Remember that the National Park Service prohibits collecting fossil wood in order to preserve the specimens that remain.

While some maps label both the huge plateau encircled by the petrified forest trails and this lower plateau as "Big Plateau," others call the upper area "Petrified Forest Plateau" and confine the name "Big Plateau" to this lower area. An older trail across Big Plateau that once headed to the north of the current trail to a now abandoned ford of the Little Missouri River north of Peaceful Valley has now been abandoned.

Our route begins a descent off Big Plateau at 8.3 miles and descends gently to close the loop at 8.8 miles (N46 57.730, W103 30.651). After crossing the Little Missouri River, return to the Peaceful Valley trailhead at 9.3 miles.

Peaceful Valley has had a long and important role in the history of Theodore Roosevelt National Park. The ranch site was originally developed in the 1880s, the same era that Roosevelt became active in the badlands. Peaceful Valley began the transition to a dude ranch in 1918. In 1936 it was sold to the government as part of what was then the Roosevelt Recreation Demonstration Area. The ranch buildings became headquarters for the Demonstration Area, and later for the Theodore Roosevelt National Memorial Park. As part of the park improvements catalyzed by Mission 66, park headquarters was moved to Medora in 1959. In 1967, the park permitted a concessionaire to use the ranch property as a base of operations for guided horseback tours. The tradition continued with various concessionaires offering trail rides through the summer of 2014.

RIGHT Wild horses are frequently found along Lower Paddock Creek.

JONES CREEK-LOWER PADDOCK CREEK TRAILS LOOP, SOUTH UNIT

A rugged circuit through the center of the South Unit for hikers or horses.

GENERAL LOCATION: Three miles north of Medora, North Dakota.

HIGHLIGHT: The wildlife watching includes bison and prairie dogs.

ACCESS: From the South Unit Medora Visitor Center, drive north on the paved Scenic Loop Drive for 8.1 miles to the parking area at the Jones Creek trailhead (N46 57.977, W103 29.229). If your group has more than one vehicle, leave one at the Halliday Well trailhead (N46 57.152, W103 29.690) (7.2 miles along the Scenic Loop Drive and 0.5 mile east) to avoid 1.5 miles of hiking along park roads.

DISTANCE: The loop is 11.4 miles around and requires a short car shuttle between trailheads. A shorter 3.0 mile out and back hike from the Halliday Well trailhead on the Lower Paddock Creek Trail offers an excellent chance to view park wildlife.

ALLOWED USES: This trail is open to hikers and horseback riders.

MAPS: USGS Theodore Roosevelt National Park South Unit 1:24,000 special topographic map, Trails Illustrated Theodore Roosevelt National Park (#259), and Map B.

One of the most popular day hike trips in Theodore Roosevelt National Park is the West Loop that connects the trails along Jones and Lower Paddock Creeks. This loop can be hiked in one long day, or it can be combined with the Upper Paddock Creek and Talkington Trails to make an overnight trip. The lower loop follows quiet creek bottoms through country much rougher than other trails in the South Unit. All trails on this loop are marked by the park's brown carsonite posts.

To hike the loop clockwise, begin by hiking east on the Jones Creek Trail and reach a trail register within 100 yards. The trail is mostly on a flat bench above creek level, but crosses the main fork of Jones Creek twice. As the trail winds along the creek bottom through green ash and grasses, notice how clusters of juniper trees are found only on the shaded and moister north-facing slopes. Just after the second crossing of Jones Creek at 1.8 miles, the Roundup Trail (N46 58.006, W103 27.157) leads left 2.1 miles to the Scenic Loop Drive. At the next junction at 2.5 miles (N46 58.029, W103 26.311), the Jones Creek Trail continues left to reach the Scenic Loop Drive in 1.0 mile. However, our route turns south with an immediate crossing of Jones Creek to follow the Lower Talkington Trail over a broad grassland that marks the divide between Jones and Paddock Creeks. On top of the grassland is an old stock pond (N46 57.488, W103 25.823) that may hold water during exceptionally wet weather. The next descent passes the stump of an outstanding preserved fossil tree and seams of lignite.

ABOVE Bluffs along Lower Paddock Creek.

Reach another signed junction at 4.3 miles (N46 5.967, W103 24.997). From here we leave the Lower Talkington Trail, which goes left to the Scenic Loop Drive in 2.3 miles, and instead turn right to follow the Badlands Spur Trail which branches south from the Lower Talkington Trail.

Follow the Badlands Spur south down a small tributary, then arc to the southwest. Along the way, pass areas where erosion of sandstone in the Bullion Creek formation has produced steep sand dunes. At 5.3 miles and just after crossing the creek, the trail closely parallels the Scenic Loop Drive. At 5.7 miles, the trail joins the Scenic Loop Drive just short of a signed pullout for the Badlands Spur (N46 56.070, W103 25.766). Follow the Scenic Loop Drive south, cross Paddock Creek, and reach the Lower Paddock Creek Trail (N46 55.918, W103 25.916) at 6.0 miles.

Turn right off the Scenic Loop Drive and follow the Lower Paddock Creek Trail downstream. Older maps may show a fork in the trail just east of the Scenic Loop Drive, but there is in fact only one main stem of the trail. The trail starts in thick sagebrush and has several closely spaced crossings of Paddock Creek, some of which can be bypassed by following informal horse trails. Notice how the meanders in Paddock Creek are tighter and more closely spaced than the meanders in the Little Missouri River. The rate of water flow in a stream, the gradient of the stream, and other properties of a watershed are related to the size of the stream. Streams cut meanders to dissipate the potential energy of water. Subsidiary streams, such as Paddock Creek, have high potential energy which is spent on cutting more frequent meanders, while main streams, such as the Little Missouri River, have less potential energy and therefore more gentle meanders. The high level of erosion in subsidiary streams means that the bed of the stream is rougher and the flow turbulent. Despite appearances, water in a turbulent, subsidiary stream flows at a slower rate than water in a larger, smooth flowing river.

At 7.3 miles, cross to the right bank of Paddock Creek. The Lower Paddock Creek Trail next passes through a remarkably large prairie dog town where bison often graze. Make another pair of creek crossings before reaching a point where the valley narrows remarkably. The rest of the trail passes through two more large prairie dog towns which provide great opportunities for wildlife watching and has some potentially muddy crossings of side creeks. At 10.0 miles there is a register box. The trail ends at 10.4 miles at the Halliday Well trailhead where there is a gravel parking area.

If you were unable to leave a second vehicle at the Halliday Well trailhead, you must walk 0.5 mile northwest along the gravel trailhead road, then 1.0 mile north along the Scenic Loop Drive to the Jones Creek trailhead. Alternatively, you can avoid the walk along the Scenic Loop Drive by walking across the Scenic Loop Drive to the Peaceful Valley Ranch Trail and taking the CCC (Civilian Conservation Corps) Trail for 0.9 mile back to the Jones Creek trailhead. Be prepared for one potentially wet creek crossing if you use the CCC Trail early in the season.

A shorter, high impact version of this hike can be had by starting at the Halliday Well trailhead and hiking out and back on the very popular first 1.5 miles of the Lower Paddock Creek Trail. Bison frequent the trailhead, along with wild horses. The first 0.4 mile passes through a huge prairie dog town, and there is another town between 0.7 and 1.4 miles. Beyond this point, the trail is less used and can be difficult to follow.

ABOVE Hiking along the Badlands Spur Trail.
RIGHT Blue Penstemon and vetch along the Roundup Trail.

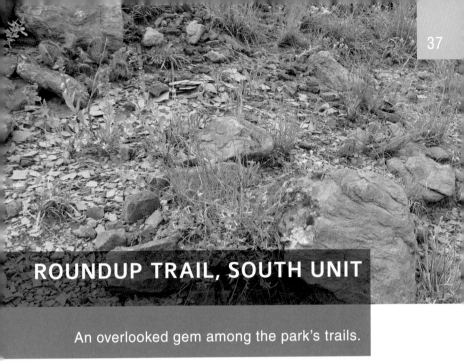

ROUNDUP TRAIL, SOUTH UNIT

An overlooked gem among the park's trails.

GENERAL LOCATION: Six miles north of Medora, North Dakota.

HIGHLIGHT: An excellent introduction to horseback
riding in the park, or an easy day hike.

ACCESS: There is no official trailhead. However, there is room
for a few cars to park at the intersection of the East River Road
and the road to Roundup Horse Camp (N47 00.139, W103
29.298). To reach the junction, leave Scenic Loop Drive at the
north end of the loop at MP 24.8 and turn north on the gravel
East River Road. In 0.8 mile, reach the signed entrance road for
Roundup Horse Camp and park on the shoulder of the road.

DISTANCE: The trail is 6.6 miles roundtrip.

ALLOWED USES: This trail is open to hikers and horseback riders.

MAPS: USGS Theodore Roosevelt National Park South
Unit 1:24,000 special topographic map, Trails Illustrated
Theodore Roosevelt National Park (#259), and Map B.

The Roundup and Mike Auney Trails were opened in 1997 primarily
to provide access to the park's trail system from the Roundup Horse
Camp on the north edge of the South Unit. But these trails are more
than just mere connectors. The Roundup Trail in particular is worth
a visit in its own right. The trail is little used but offers outstanding

vistas across the grasslands and to the small scattered buttes that dot the north edge of the park. The trail is marked by the park's brown carsonite posts.

The Roundup Trail starts at the intersection of the East River and Roundup Camp roads. There are no trailhead signs here, but the first post leading east across the grassland is visible from the road. This is good habitat for pronghorn, and these speedy ungulates aren't afraid to show themselves by walking along the prairie ridgetops. The trail drops into a tree-lined draw before climbing within a few feet of a corner of the park boundary fence.

At 1.2 miles (N46 59.490, W103 28.268), the trail crosses Scenic Loop Drive at the road's milepost 24, then makes a normally easy crossing of the scoria-lined bottom of Jules Creek. At 2.1 miles, reach the crest of a ridge where a prairie dog town is visible on the valley floor to the west. The trail follows this crest with outstanding views. At 2.5 miles (N46 58.589, W103 27.674), reach the site of a long-abandoned stock pond that may have water after heavy rains. Horses can easily access the pond, but riders should be aware that the pond will be dry under most conditions.

South of the pond the trail reaches the end of the ridge and descends to reach the signed junction with the Jones Creek Trail (N46 58.006, W103 27.157) at 3.3 miles, just east of where Jones Creek Trail crosses its namesake creek. From this point it is 1.7 miles west on the Jones Creek Trail to the Scenic Loop Drive near Peaceful Valley and 0.7 mile east on the Jones Creek Trail to the junction with the Lower Talkington Trail. Retrace your route to complete the hike.

ABOVE Small bands of wild horses roam the Theodore Roosevelt backcountry.
RIGHT Descending from Buck Hill.

UPPER PADDOCK CREEK UPPER TALKINGTON TRAILS LOOP, SOUTH UNIT

A long loop on lesser used trails
for experienced hikers.

GENERAL LOCATION: Seven miles northeast of Medora, North Dakota.

HIGHLIGHT: The wildlife watching includes wild horses and bison.

ACCESS: Exit Interstate 94 at Medora and proceed to the
South Unit Visitor Center in Medora. From the visitor center,
follow the paved Scenic Loop Drive counterclockwise for 14.7
miles to the Badlands Spur trailhead (N46 56.070, W103 25.766)
on the left side past where Paddock Creek and its namesake
trails cross the Scenic Loop Drive.

DISTANCE: A 16.4-mile loop. A shorter loop from Buck Hill involving
some cross-country hiking and road walking is 11.3 miles long.

ALLOWED USES: This trail is open to hikers and horseback riders.

MAPS: USGS Theodore Roosevelt National Park South
Unit 1:24,000 special topographic map, Trails Illustrated
Theodore Roosevelt National Park (#259), and Map B.

The Upper Talkington and Upper Paddock Creek Trails combine with
the Badlands Spur and Rim trails to form the East Loop, giving hikers
and horseback riders the chance to combine some of the park's most
rugged scenery with primetime wildlife watching. This little used loop
can be done as a long day trip or overnight backpack trip. Hikers should
be aware that portions of the loop can be difficult to follow.

To hike the East Loop counterclockwise from the Badlands Spur trailhead, begin by walking the park scenic road south back to the crossing of Paddock Creek at 0.3 mile and the junction with the Upper Paddock Creek Trail. The Upper Paddock Creek Trail is marked by the park's large wooden posts. Next, turn left and east to follow the south side of Paddock Creek (N46 55.756, W103 25.597) upstream to a crossing at 0.7 mile that can be wet early in the season. Once across, the trail continues following the north side of the wide valley of Paddock Creek. Though wedged between the creek and the badlands that surround it, the trail here can be difficult to follow. Numerous bison trails cross the official trail route and the tall wooden posts are often knocked over by bison scratching on them. If you lose the trail at any point in the first three miles, just continue west along the north bank of the creek to encounter it again.

This valley is also one of the favorite hangouts for the park's wild horses. If you spot a herd, look for the lead stallion working to keep the group together. The park's feral horses descend from domesticated animals that escaped into the wild. Early in the history of the park, attempts were made to remove horses. However, in 1970 the park decided to manage them as part of the historical setting, consistent with conditions during Roosevelt's time. There are now around 140 horses roaming free in the South Unit. An excellent resource for tracking the park's horses in the North Dakota Badlands Horse web site at: www.ndbh.org.

ABOVE A wild horse colt running in the meadow.

Deer, grouse, and bison are commonly seen on this loop. In fact, it is best to allow a little extra time and energy on this loop for detouring around groups of bison. As my wife opined after another long detour, "Your mileage may vary."

After pulling north away from the creek, reach a signpost marking the intersection with the Painted Canyon Trail at 3.6 miles (N46 54.678, W103 23.511), just after crossing a major side creek coming in from the north. The Painted Canyon Trail will lead right 2.1 miles to the visitor center located on the canyon rim while the East Loop continues straight ahead. The lush high grass along the trail here supports one of the park's densest tick populations, so be sure to check your skin and clothing frequently. Though the trail now is marked by the standard carsonite posts, many of the older 6" x 6" wooden bison posts can be found discarded along the route. You may spot small groups of bison lounging in the shade of small buttes.

After crossing a shallow draw, the trail next reaches open woods around the Southeast Corner Spring at 6.8 miles (N46 53.836, W103 19.651) where the trail beyond is now called the Rim Trail. If you choose to use water from the spring for drinking, remember that it must be treated. From the wooded grove, the trail swings south of a draw containing two old stock tanks.

Next the trail reaches the gentle grasslands near the southeast corner of the park. Up on the grasslands, development around the Fryburg Exit off Interstate 94 is visible just across the park's perimeter fence. The trail turns due north across the grasslands, but the exact route is difficult to follow as there is often no beaten path or trail posts to be found due to bison activity. At 8.9 miles, intersect the Upper Talkington Trail (W103 19.303) near a pair of trail posts at the head of a major draw leading west to a prairie dog town. Finding this intersection is one of the cases in the park where navigation by GPS is particularly helpful. After a short descent, reach a huge prairie dog town.

Beyond the prairie dog town, the trail is well-marked, the grade is level, and the walking fast. As the trail winds to the northwest, look for cannonball formations in some eroding rock outcrops and for bison grazing below a few of the teepee-shaped buttes. At 12.7 miles, cross the Scenic Loop Drive (N46 56.315, W103 22.845) at the signed Talkington trailhead and continue west on the Lower Talkington Trail. The trail crosses a small prairie dog town, then follows a small creek valley, and then climbs to reach the junction with the Badlands Spur Trail at 15.0 miles (N46 56.967, W103 24.997). Turn left as the Badlands Spur Trail traverses mostly south across open grassland before approaching the Scenic Loop Drive and reaching its trailhead at the end of the loop at 16.4 miles.

For those planning to stay overnight on this loop, finding water will be a problem. Southeast Corner Spring could be used, but this water is not dependable and should be treated before drinking. Paddock Creek often contains many pools of water, but this source is unappetizing at best.

Those experienced in off-trail travel and looking for a shorter loop can make an 11.3-mile loop by starting at the end of the Buck Hill Trail, travelling cross country south to the Upper Paddock Creek Trail, and combining the Upper Paddock Creek, Rim, and Upper Talkington Trails with a return via the Scenic Loop Drive and Buck Hill Roads. From the Buck Hill trailhead (N46 55.588, W103 23.374), follow the Buck Hill Trail 0.2 mile to the top of Buck Hill. A prominent ridge leads almost due south (and in line with the Painted Canyon Visitor Center on the horizon) from Buck Hill. The upper slopes of Buck Hill are grassy and you may find an obvious rock circle at 0.6 mile. From this point, the route steepens as it follows a series of rough game paths down to the valley floor. There are a few steep pitches on the descent, but you should reach the Upper Paddock Creek Trail in 1.3 miles at a point about 0.6 mile west of the junction with the Painted Canyon Trail (N46 54.741, W103 23.158).

On your return, exit the Upper Talkington Trail at the point where it crosses the loop road. Walk 0.5 mile west on the Scenic Loop Drive to the Buck Hill Road, then climb the final 0.8 miles back to the Buck Hill trailhead to complete the 11.3-mile loop.

ABOVE Wild horses grazing under the passing noonday clouds.
RIGHT Gumbo lily, or evening primrose, is common in the badlands.

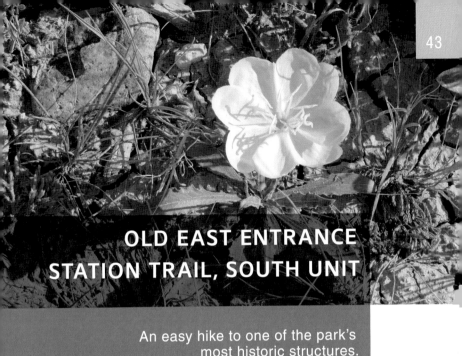

OLD EAST ENTRANCE STATION TRAIL, SOUTH UNIT

An easy hike to one of the park's most historic structures.

GENERAL LOCATION: Four miles east of Medora, North Dakota.

HIGHLIGHT: The incredibly detailed CCC-era stone- and ironwork in these historic structures.

ACCESS: Follow the Scenic Loop Drive to MP 12.9 and park in the small pullout (N46 54.743, W103 25.741).

DISTANCE: This hike is 1.0 mile roundtrip.

ALLOWED USES: This trail is open to hikers only.

MAPS: USGS Theodore Roosevelt National Park South Unit 1:24,000 special topographic map, Trails Illustrated Theodore Roosevelt National Park (#259), and Map B.

The Old East Entrance Station Trail provides a short walk to one of the park's most historic structures. If you look closely from the pullout, you can see the station in the distance partly obscured by trees. The trail to it is the most recent addition to the park trail system. The trail starts on the south side of a small butte, and almost immediately the well-defined trail enters a small prairie dog town. Just after leaving the prairie dog town, you see the two remaining sandstone structures ahead (N46 54.516, W103 25.318).

The East Entrance Station was completed in 1938 by the CCC (Civilian Conservation Corps) and originally consisted of the two remaining buildings, the check station and privy, and a third structure called the pylon (the large stone Theodore Roosevelt National Park monument). The pylon was moved to Painted Canyon Overlook in 1968 after the completion of Interstate 94 and the abandonment of the old entrance. The small sandstone check station and gate are still remarkably well-preserved in their original locations, and details of the intricate ironwork and stone carving are still visible.

The check station is a marvel of meticulous construction. The stonework is exceptionally detailed with casement windows and fine chiseling on the interior surfaces. The initials AFB carved into a decorative stone above the fireplace indicate that much of the stonework may have been done by Arthur Boicourt, one of the local craftsmen contracted to work with the CCC crews.

The ironwork exposed on the outside of the check station is remarkable as well. According to the park's 1980 historic structures report, the work was done by Einer Olstad, a blacksmith and rancher from Medora, who worked with the Works Progress Administration (WPA). Much of the ironwork is incised with the figures of Roosevelt's Maltese Cross and Elkhorn ranch brands.

Opposite the check station stands the abandoned privy. Stone walls extend from both structures and led to wooden fences when the station was in use. Today, little remains of the original entry road that separates the two buildings, and it is difficult to imagine this location as the main park entrance.

The replacement of the Old East Entrance Station was only a small part of a much larger National Park Service revitalization effort called Mission 66. Most park visitors have heard the story of the role of the Civilian Conservation Corps in building much of the infrastructure of America's parks, but few are aware of the tremendous role that Mission 66 had in creating the modern parks. At Theodore Roosevelt, the changes brought by Mission 66 were huge. Park headquarters was moved from an antiquated location at Peaceful Valley Ranch to newly acquired property on the current site in Medora. The new South Unit entrance road was built from Medora to Peaceful Valley, and a west entrance, requiring a ford of the Little Missouri River, was closed. Roosevelt's Maltese Cross Cabin was moved onto the Medora site and underwent a historical reconstruction. By 1963, construction of Interstate 94 triggered changes to the eastern entrance. The interstate's construction, surfacing, and new overpass between 1964 and 1966 mandated closing the historic east entrance and the reroute of park traffic through Medora. Today, traffic through the Old East Entrance Station is limited to periodic visits from wildlife and occasional groups of curious hikers.

ABOVE The old East Entrance Station in Theodore Roosevelt NP.

PETRIFIED FOREST TRAILS LOOP, SOUTH UNIT

A long day hike into the South Unit, which features fossils and plentiful wildlife watching.

GENERAL LOCATION: Three miles north of Medora, North Dakota.

HIGHLIGHT: Petrified trees, bison, and prairie dog watching in a wilderness setting.

ACCESS: To reach the Petrified Forest trailhead, pick up a copy of the map and directions at the South Unit Visitor Center. Then take Exit 23 off Interstate 94. Drive north on DPG Road 730, which is the West River Road for 2.5 miles and keep left at a junction with a ranch road. Much of the next section of road crosses private land, but public access is allowed on the road. At 5.0 miles, turn right onto DPG 730-2 which is signed for the Petrified Forest, then left at the next junction at 5.2 miles. Keep left at the next junction at 5.5 miles to reach the signed trailhead at 5.7 miles (N46 59.763, W103 36.290). The gravel roads on this access route typically are suitable for passenger cars.

DISTANCE: The Petrified Forest Trails combine with the Maah Daah Hey Trail for a 10.4-mile loop. There are exposures of the petrified forest on both the North and South Petrified Forest Trails. Each exposure can be visited in a three-mile roundtrip hike.

ALLOWED USES: This trail is open to hikers and horseback riders.

MAPS: USGS Theodore Roosevelt National Park South Unit 1:24,000 special topographic map, Trails Illustrated Theodore Roosevelt National Park (#259), and Map B.

LEFT Tree stumps are the most common fossil along the Petrified Forest Loop.
ABOVE The Petrified Forest Trailhead.

The Petrified Forest loop on the west side of the South Unit of
Theodore Roosevelt National Park combines two areas of special
interest, the badlands containing the Petrified Forest Plateau and
the grasslands, seemingly teeming with wildlife that surround them.
Despite the relatively out of the way route to the trailhead, this is one
of the park's most popular hikes.

From the trailhead, cross through a self-closing gate and then pass
a trail register. The trail climbs gently to the plateau through a mix of
badlands and grasslands dotted with flowers such as flax, textile onion,
and spurge. If this section of the trail is wet and difficult to hike, it is
wise to abort the hike as the petrified forest locations are surrounded by
gumbo, which can be impassable when wet.

Reach the start of the loop at 0.5 mile at the signed junction with
the North and South Petrified Forest Trails (N46 59.823, W103 36.683).
To hike the loop clockwise, turn left to follow the North Petrified
Forest Trail. Drop off the grassland to reach the start of the Petrified
Forest at 1.3 miles. It is a rare privilege to visit so amazing a fossil
site. Within the thick layer of bentonite are the bleached remains of
the stumps of dozens of large trees, with much of their original texture
still preserved 55 million years later. Odd sandstone concretions mix

ABOVE Approaching the Maah Daah Hey Trail junction.

among the fossils, and harder silt and sandstone layers form many of the caprocks so distinctive in the badlands.

Exit the far end of the forest for the short climb back up to the plateau grassland. As you approach the north end of the loop, you'll descend off the plateau to cross a shallow creek which may contain pools of water. At the top of the climb out on a badlands ridge, reach the junction with the Maah Daah Hey (MDH) Trail at 3.3 miles (N47 01.314, W103 33.538). To the left, the MDH leaves the park, and then intersects the north end of the Buffalo Gap Trail in 0.5 mile. Our route will turn right and follow the Maah Daah Hey Trail to the south.

The next five miles are some of the easiest and most pleasurable walking imaginable as the trail traverses the level east rim of Big Plateau and then turns west to reenter the Petrified Forest. The handy Maah Daah Hey mileposts will help you gauge your progress across the grassland, but don't be too distracted by the Little Missouri River views or the diverse grasslands wildflowers to overlook the bison, wild horses, and pronghorn that roam the plateau. Look for a small prairie dog town between mileposts 59 and 58. At 6.2 miles (N46 59.205, W103 32.476), reach the signed junction with the Mike Auney Trail on the left which leads east across the Little Missouri River to the Roundup Horse Camp.

At 6.6 miles, reach the V-shaped junction with the South Petrified Forest Trail (N46 58.931, W103 32.265). From this point, the Maah Daah Hey Trail continues south for 0.2 mile to Big Plateau Junction, while our route takes a very sharp right turn to follow the South Petrified Forest Trail, again passing a small prairie dog town. Make sure to head west northwest on the correct path, as marker posts are rare in this section. At 7.6 miles (N46 59.244, W103 33.370), reach the signed junction with the Lone Tree Loop Trail which joins from the left.

From the Lone Tree junction, it is another mile before the trail descends to reenter the Petrified Forest. Again, the concentration of fossils in this location is wonderous. The largest fossil here is almost 12 feet long, but there are dozens of fossilized stumps to examine. The trail will then return to the plateau top and close the loop at 9.9 miles (N46 59.823, W103 36.683). Rehike the 0.5-mile long entry trail to return to the trailhead.

If you want to complete an off-trail hike via the Little Missouri River, leave the Maah Daah Hey Trail near the north boundary of the park where the trail turns south and hike northeast down a series of bluffs to the river bottom. A fine cluster of fossilized stumps sits nearby on a small bench just below the level of the trail. An easy descent route follows a long-abandoned jeep track along the nose of a small ridge before dropping into a small draw. Two groves of cottonwoods between the north boundary of the park and VA well offer campsites.

A riverside camp has the advantage of water otherwise unavailable in the backcountry. The wells found scattered throughout the park are water sources for wildlife and do not produce potable water, so treatment is necessary. An added bonus is that the river, which seemed so cold when you waded across it in the morning, could be warm enough for swimming by afternoon. The bluffs on either side of the river are perfect for wildlife watching or photography.

On the second day, follow the river upstream for five miles back to Peaceful Valley, crossing the Mike Auney Trail. Bluffs along the river can be climbed or bypassed by wading in the river. Pass through another huge prairie dog town at Beef Corral Bottom. Beyond the prairie dog town, cross the river once more to avoid bushwhacking along the narrow strip between the river and the paved park road. End your hike at the Peaceful Valley Ranch parking area.

The rocks in Theodore Roosevelt National Park originally were deposited as sediments during the Paleocene epoch (55-65 million years ago). Rocks of the Bullion Creek (also called Tongue River) and Sentinel Butte formations, which are both part of the Fort Union Group, are found. These sediments were deposited by the rivers and streams that drained the ancestral Rocky Mountains to the west. At this distance from the mountains, the streams carried clay, silt, and sand which are now the soft siltstone and sandstone beds of the Fort Union Group. As the ancient Rocky Mountains began to rise, a chain of volcanoes became active in what is now Montana and Wyoming. Huge eruptions of these volcanoes sent ash as far east as the Dakotas. These ash deposits are found in the park as beds of bentonite, the clay mineral commonly called gumbo when wet. Bentonite has the remarkable ability to absorb five times its weight in water. Even more remarkable is how difficult bentonite is to walk on, or drive over, when wet. Gumbo is extremely sticky and slippery at the same time. There is no cure, only prevention; it is best to stay out of the badlands after a recent rain.

Paleontological excavations by the North Dakota Geological Survey in the Sentinel Butte and Bullion Creek formations have discovered fossils of a 55-million-year-old crocodile-like reptile called *Champosaurus*. To learn more about the dig and the park's rich fossil history, visit the paleontology exhibit at the Medora Visitor Center.

Petrified wood is common throughout Theodore Roosevelt National Park. The rapid rate of Paleocene sedimentation accounts for the formation of fossil wood. In the Paleocene climate, much of the landscape was covered by thick forests and swamps. After rapid changes in stream channels or volcanic eruptions, many trees were buried before they decayed. Following further burial, groundwater began to circulate through the sediments. Silica that was dissolved from the ash beds was then redeposited in the wood as groundwater saturated the buried trees. Eventually, silica replaced and coated much of the woody plant tissues to create petrified wood. In well-preserved specimens, growth rings and other features still are visible. The most common type of petrified wood in the park is preserved tree stumps.

ABOVE Dramatic summer skies on the Petrified Forest Trail Loop.

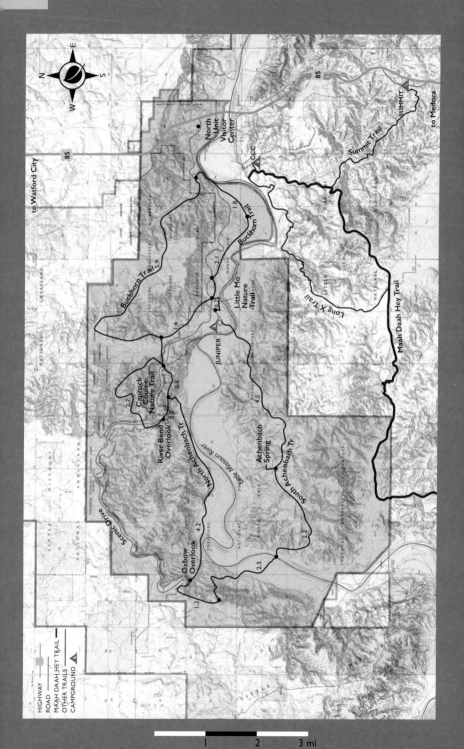

N E S W

85

to Watford City

LITTLE MISSOURI NATIONAL GRASSLAND

85

North Unit Visitor Center

to Medora

to Summit

SUMMIT

Summit Trail

CCC

Buckhorn Trail 5.9

Buckhorn Trail

1.8

2.1

Little Mo Nature Trail

0.2

Long X Trail

LITTLE MISSOURI NATIONAL

Maah Daah Hey Trail

1.6

JUNIPER

Caprock Coulee Nature Trail

2.7

0.8

North Achenbach Tr

4.5

Achenbach Spring

South Achenbach Tr

River Bend Overlook 0.6

Little Missouri River

Scenic Drive

4.2

Oxbow Overlook

2.2

2.5

1.2

LITTLE MISSOURI NATIONAL GRASSLAND

HIGHWAY
ROAD
MAÄH DAAH HEY TRAIL
OTHER TRAILS
CAMPGROUND

1   2   3 mi

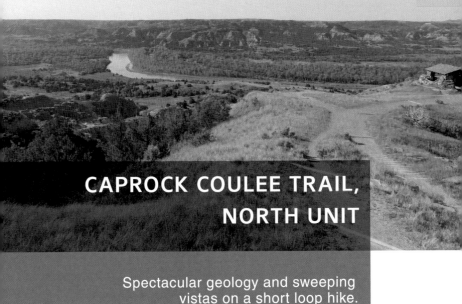

CAPROCK COULEE TRAIL, NORTH UNIT

Spectacular geology and sweeping vistas on a short loop hike.

GENERAL LOCATION: Thirteen miles south of Watford City, North Dakota.

HIGHLIGHT: The first 0.8 mile of this loop is a self-guided nature trail.

ACCESS: From US 85, drive 6.5 miles west on the paved Scenic Drive to Caprock Coulee Nature Trail Pullout on the north side of the road (N47 36.595, W103 21.350).

DISTANCE: The loop is 4.1 miles around.

ALLOWED USES: This trail is open to hikers only.

MAPS: USGS Theodore Roosevelt National Park North Unit 1:24,000 special topographic map, Trails Illustrated Theodore Roosevelt National Park (#259), and Map C.

If you have time for only one hike in the North Unit of Theodore Roosevelt National Park, it should be the Caprock Coulee Trail. The first part (0.8 mile) of this trail is a self-guided introduction to the geology and botany of the badlands and prairie. Be sure to pick up a copy of the

ABOVE Riverbend Overlook is the most scenic place in the North Unit.

self-guiding brochure at the trailhead. This brochure does as good a job as I've seen anywhere of raising the hiker's appreciation for the biology and geology of an area. Beyond the self-guided portion lies some of the best ridgeline walking found in the park. This trail is closed to horses.

Follow the numbered posts north from the trailhead along Caprock Coulee. At 0.1 mile, a connector trail splits right to intersect the Buckhorn Trail in 0.3 mile. You'll soon reach a register box and will hike north with an imposing badlands wall on your right. If you plan to hike the North Unit's longer trails later in your trip, pay attention to the guide's descriptions of the three types of sagebrush that occur in the park and see if you can find and identify all three types based on the shape of their leaves. At the end of the self-guided portion at 0.8 mile (N47 37.139, W103 21.563), turn west, then south, follow the carsonite posts to climb through some badlands, and then up through a grove of juniper and green ash. Western wheatgrass is the dominant grass in these groves. The trail turns west again at the top of a narrow ridge. At 1.6 miles enjoy a comfortable bench at a scenic vista. Follow the ridge west as it widens into open prairie before crossing the paved Scenic Drive at 2.5 miles (N47 36.742, W103 22.781).

Follow the Scenic Drive south to Riverbend Overlook (N47 35.593, W103 22.672) at 2.7 miles where a side trail leads south to the

ABOVE Scenic badlands along the Caprock Coulee Trail.

magnificent CCC-built stone shelter perched invitingly above the Little Missouri River. The trail exits along the side of the pullout's guardrail, stays on the roadside, and crosses the heads of two small coulees. Then, turn right off the road onto the crest of a ridge leading east. Keep left at a junction with the North Achenbach Trail (N47 36.488, W103 22.243) at 3.1 miles and continue east along an especially scenic ridgeline. Along the way, pass unusual log-shaped sandstone concretions. Cross two small saddles offering spectacular views of the Little Missouri River before turning north off the ridge. Descend steadily on switchbacks to return to the trailhead at 4.1 miles.

The diversity of the Caprock Coulee Trail makes it an ideal introduction to Theodore Roosevelt National Park. The trail crosses most of the park's major habitats: sharp-edged coulees, juniper groves, narrow badlands ridges, and open prairie. The views are superb, particularly on the south side where the trail overlooks the Little Missouri River. Coyotes, mule deer, and rabbits find the trail easy going, and you may also see tracks from one of the park's rare bobcats.

The display of geologic features along the trail is also impressive. On the self-guided portion, you'll learn how water erodes soft bedrock to create badlands. You will see examples of lignite seams, bentonite beds, landslides, slump blocks, and caprocks.

Theodore Roosevelt National Park personnel, along with assistance from the North Dakota Fish and Game Department and researchers from Montana State University, began an effort to introduce bighorn sheep into the North Unit in 1996. Native Audubon bighorns became extinct in the early 1900s from hunting pressure and loss of habitat. An effort by the North Dakota Fish and Game Department to transplant California bighorn sheep into the Little Missouri badlands began outside of the park in 1956 and eventually included the South Unit. The earlier effort resulted in a stable herd of around 250 sheep. However, the historic sheep range in the North Unit of Theodore Roosevelt was unoccupied until 19 California bighorns were released into the park in 1996.

Eight lambs were born the first year and seven more were born in 1997. The band mingles with other groups living outside the park. The North Dakota Game and Fish Department estimates that there were approximately 20 bighorn sheep in the park in 2018 with an additional 280 in other parts of the state. Theodore Roosevelt National Park has a long history of successful wildlife reintroductions, which includes bison in 1956 and elk in 1985.

There is no water on the Caprock Coulee Nature Trail, and you'll probably appreciate a refreshing drink after being exposed to North Dakota's special combination of sun and wind. In winter, the Scenic Drive is open as far as the Caprock Coulee Nature trailhead.

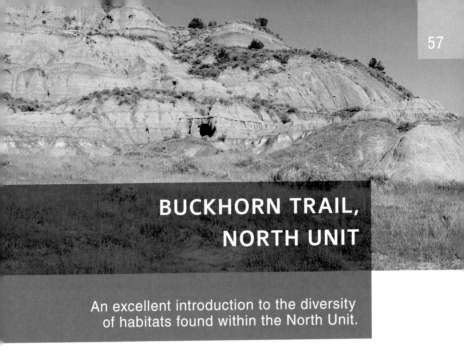

BUCKHORN TRAIL, NORTH UNIT

An excellent introduction to the diversity of habitats found within the North Unit.

GENERAL LOCATION: Thirteen miles south of Watford City, North Dakota.

HIGHLIGHT: The wildlife watching includes a large prairie dog town, bison, and longhorn cattle.

ACCESS: From US 85, drive 4.9 miles west on the paved Scenic Drive to the Cannonball Concretions Pullout (N47 35.785, W103 19.947) which is located directly opposite the entrance to the Juniper Campground.

DISTANCE: An 11.4-mile loop open to hikers and horses. With a car shuttle you can skip the last four miles of the trail that closely parallel the Scenic Drive.

ALLOWED USES: This trail is open to hikers and horses.

MAPS: USGS Theodore Roosevelt National Park North Unit 1:24,000 special topographic map, Trails Illustrated Theodore Roosevelt National Park (#259), and Map C.

The Buckhorn Trail is an ideal introduction to the diversity of habitats found in the North Unit of Theodore Roosevelt National Park. Along the way, hikers will visit immense prairie dog towns, pass herds

LEFT Wildflowers along the Caprock Coulee trail.
ABOVE Hiking across the Squaw Creek Valley.

of bison, and may even spot part of the park's small herd of Texas longhorn cattle. The terrain along the loop includes open prairie, high tablelands, and narrow canyons carved into steep slopes.

From the pullout, start north along the base of a small badlands cliff to hike the loop clockwise and reach a register box at 0.2 mile. The trail is marked by a variety of wooden and carsonite posts. At 1.6 miles (N47 36.638, W103 20.960), reach a junction with a side trail that leads left for 0.3 mile to the Caprock Coulee Nature Trail. Keep right at the junction and you will cross a small draw at 2.1 miles and enter a large prairie dog town where bison may also be seen. The NPS has marked the north end of the dog town at 2.8 miles. The hike to the end of the dog town is a popular short hike, and the trail beyond is much less used and harder to follow.

The Squaw Creek valley north of the town also is favored by bison, so be careful not to surprise these giants. Bison are the largest mammal in North America: Bulls can reach a height of six feet at the shoulder and weigh up to 2,600 pounds. The smaller females can still reach an impressive five feet six inches and 1,100 pounds. The slaughter of the great bison herds in the late 1800s is a shameful story we all know well. By the time these magnificent animals were protected in the late 1890s, only a few hundred remained in the wild. But bison have proved to be resilient, and once again they thrive in their native habitat. In 1956, 29 bison were brought to the South Unit from Fort Niobrara National Wildlife Refuge in Nebraska. This herd did well enough to seed the North Unit herd with 10 bulls and 10 cows in 1962. Though both units of the park could carry larger numbers of bison, park managers currently have set herd sizes at approximately

ABOVE Prairie dog watching is a favorite perennial activity.

200 to 400 animals for the South Unit and 100 to 300 for the North Unit to maintain healthy range conditions.

Leave the valley of Squaw Creek where the trail turns northeast and proceed up a small valley with abundant trees and shade. Make a sharp turn to the southeast and keep a careful lookout for trail posts protruding from the deep sagebrush. But sage isn't the only plant in this valley—chokecherry, textile onion, and dandelion also can be found. When the valley splits, the trail follows the right side of the left fork. At 3.7 miles (N47 37.317, W103 20.211), begin climbing through layers of concretions, bentonite, scoria, and petrified wood. Climb through a grove of juniper to reach an open plateau at 4.4 miles (N47 37.013, W103 19.521) with some of the park's farthest views.

Near the end of the plateau, pass a small prairie dog town on the right of the trail. The descent from the plateau starting at 5.5 miles (N47 36.536, W103 18.354) is perhaps even more scenic than the views from the top of it. You'll make two crossings of an unnamed creek that is favored by mule deer before climbing along the west side of the creek. At 7.5 miles (N47 36.053, W103 16.769), reach the Scenic Drive just to the west of a bridge over the creek. Beyond the crossing of the Scenic Drive, the Buckhorn Trail is much less scenic. If possible, consider a 3.6-mile car shuttle, or road walk back to the trailhead.

If not using a shuttle, cross the road and follow a narrow strip between the road and a fence along the edge of the bluff high above the Little Missouri River. In 0.5 mile, you'll reach the spacious bottomland where the river rounds a wide meander. Watch here for large herds of bison and the park's demonstration herd of Texas longhorn cattle. It is more important to give these animals a wide berth than to follow the scattered signposts that mark the trail. At 9.3 miles (N47 35.186, W103 18.015), reach a gravel road that leads to the park's bison management corral.

As you continue northwest, keep a careful lookout for the trail posts which may be hiding behind tall sagebrush or knocked over by scratching bison. The trail skirts the loop road and then leaves the river bottomland. Note the effects that fire has had on sagebrush. New bushes spring from the charred remains of those consumed in a controlled burn. The park has an active prescribed burning program with a goal to treat 1,000 to 2,000 acres yearly.

As you climb over a small saddle, notice a small pond on the left. The final section of trail involves crossing the road to the Juniper Campground's waste facility and two crossings of the Little Mo Nature Trail (N47 35.678, W103 19.621). After the second crossing of the nature trail at 11.2 miles, follow a two-track dirt road back to the trailhead at 11.4 miles.

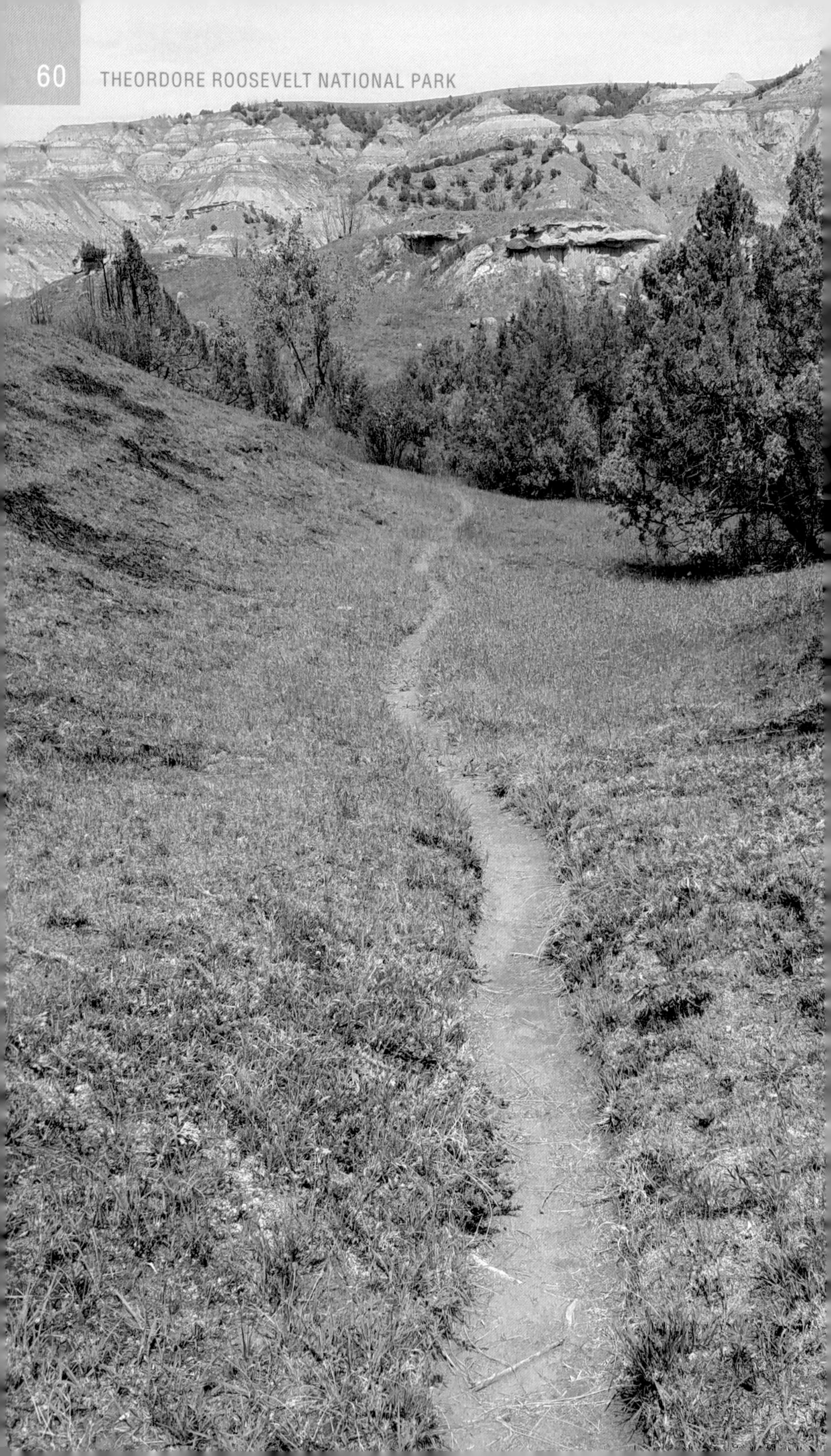

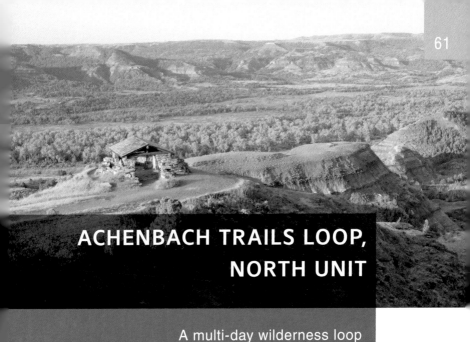

ACHENBACH TRAILS LOOP, NORTH UNIT

A multi-day wilderness loop
for hikers and horseback riders.

GENERAL LOCATION: Fourteen miles south of Watford
City, North Dakota.

HIGHLIGHT: Wilderness solitude along the Little Missouri River.

ACCESS: From US 85, drive 4.9 miles west on the paved Scenic
Drive. Turn south onto the road to Juniper Campground for 0.4
mile (N47 35.582, W103 20.345). The Achenbach Trail starts
where the road bends right to turn into the campground.

DISTANCE: Use parts of the Caprock Coulee and
Buckhorn trails to form a 19.3-mile loop.

ALLOWED USES: This trail is open to hikers and horses.

MAPS: USGS Theodore Roosevelt National Park North
Unit 1:24,000 special topographic map, Trails Illustrated
Theodore Roosevelt National Park (#259), and Map C.

The Achenbach Trail explores some of the roughest and most remote
terrain found in Theodore Roosevelt National Park. In the park's
North Unit, the elevation difference between the upper grasslands

LEFT Remnants of a grassland fire along the Achenbach Trail.
ABOVE Riverbend Overlook along the North Unit Scenic Drive.

and the river bottom is greater, and the terrain is more rugged than in the South Unit. Except for a narrow corridor around the park's Scenic Drive, most of the North Unit is designated wilderness. Through the heart of this country is a loop that is long enough for a two- or three-day trip. Before attempting to cross the Little Missouri River, check with the park staff on current conditions to determine if river levels are low enough to ford safely.

From Juniper Campground, hike 0.2 mile southwest, past a register box to the Little Missouri River. Ford the river (N47 35.496, W103 20.740) and then cross the floodplain before climbing through a mixture of badlands and juniper groves. Once onto the prairie above the river, follow the South Achenbach Trail west, and then south to a point near the park boundary. Continue west on a north-facing slope to reach a junction with an old two-track road that leads southeast to the park boundary. Then, enter the Achenbach Hills and reach a junction with a side trail leading north to Achenbach Spring, a source of nonpotable water, at 4.7 miles.

Continue across the Achenbach Hills through open prairie. Descend gradually to reach the Little Missouri River at 6.9 miles (N47 34.458, W103 26.155). Take special care to follow the trail along the river bottom and across the river. Campsites can be found in the cottonwoods along the river. Once across the river, enter some woods at 7.1 miles and encounter a swampy section on the far side of the woods. Beyond the swamp (which is likely to have dried up late in the season), cross a flat section of the river bottom where the trail posts may be obscured by large sagebrush. At 7.7 miles (N47 34.987,

ABOVE Hiking the grassland near Sperati Point.

W103 26.503), the trail reaches the edge of the badlands by the mouth of a small draw. Continue north along the edge of the badlands until the trail turns left (N47 35.345, W103 26.380) at 8.2 miles to begin the climb to Sperati Point. The climb offers a little shade and a lot of gumbo, which is best avoided when wet. Reach the junction with the 0.1-mile spur trail to Sperati Point at 9.4 miles (N47 35.716, W103 26.914). The side trail is short, but the vistas from it do not differ much from the scenery available on the climb from the river.

The prairie top section is well-defined, marked by short wooden posts, and continues the scenic vistas of the Little Missouri River. There is a register box shortly before reaching a trailhead at Oxbow Overlook at 10.6 miles (N47 36.200, W103 26.545). Overnight hikers may be able to cache water near here. Beyond Oxbow Overlook, follow the North Achenbach Trail through an exposed cut in the steep slope just below the overlook. Then descend steadily back down to the river bottom through some rock layers that contain fossil wood. Reach the north edge of the river bottom at 11.2 miles (N47 35.894, W103 26.057) and continue to follow the edge upstream and to the east. Shortly, you will cross a dry wash and enter a grove of cottonwoods that offer appealing camping. The traverse of the river bottom to the northeast requires some vigilant searching for the wooden trail posts, especially in the areas where the sagebrush is tall.

At 14.0 miles, climb out of the river bottom, then cross Appel Creek at 14.5 miles (N47 36.215, W103 23.181). The trail can be hard to follow in the broken terrain beyond Appel Creek, but the climb is well-marked back up to the rim at 15.7 miles (N47 36.324, W103 22.154). The climb has two steep sections and reaches a junction with the Caprock Coulee Trail at 16.0 miles (N47 36.488, W103 22.243). It is 0.4 mile left on the Caprock Coulee Trail to the Scenic Drive at Riverbend Overlook, but our route continues right. Ahead is a spectacular ridge crest section with continuous river views that reaches the Caprock Coulee trailhead (N47 36.595, W103 21.320) at 17.0 miles.

From the Caprock Coulee trailhead follow the connector trail for 0.3 mile east to the Buckhorn Trail (N47 36.638, W103 20.960) at 17.3 miles. Turn right and south to follow the Buckhorn Trail back to its trailhead at the Cannonball Concretions Pullout at 18.9 miles (N47 35.783, W103 19.948). To close the loop, walk the Juniper Campground road back to the Achenbach trailhead at 19.3 miles.

Luckily for the hikers that do not have the time to hike the full loop, or arrive when the flow in the Little Missouri is too high to cross, there are two shorter options from the Oxbow Overlook. From the overlook, hikers can walk 1.2 miles west across the prairie to the overlook at Sperati Point, and another 2.5 miles down to the Little

Missouri River for a 7.4 mile roundtrip hike that includes the wildlife watching on the prairie, a rugged descent through the badlands, and a hike along the bottomland to the river. Hikers can also leave Oxbow Overlook to the east and descend 0.6 mile through spectacular badlands down to the river bottom and back for a 1.2 mile roundtrip.

In hot weather, access to the cool water of the Little Missouri River is a luxury for most travelers. Neither river crossing on the loop hike is normally difficult. However, the river can be hazardous or impossible to cross if the level is high. The water usually is less than knee deep, although it can be much higher. The warm, silty water isn't ideal for a midday swim, but you can cool off by wallowing in some of the deeper pools. Channel catfish, goldeye shiners, and flathead chub live in the river.

As with any hike in the badlands, you may confuse your trail with those made by bison. Carry a compass and topographic map on this loop and know how to use them. This is a good area to watch wildlife, particularly wild turkeys, but you may also encounter ticks, prairie rattlesnakes, and poison ivy. There is no drinking water along this loop, so carry your own. If you must drink from the silty Little Missouri River, filter the water with a unit designed to remove giardia bacteria. To save wear on your filter and pump, prefilter with a double layer of coffee filters, or let the water settle overnight.

ABOVE Wild horses are easy to see in the South Unit.

OTHER THEODORE ROOSEVELT NATIONAL PARK TRAILS

PAINTED CANYON NATURE TRAIL The popular *Painted Canyon Nature Trail* (0.9 mile, South Unit) leaves from the picnic area near the Painted Canyon Visitor Center at Exit 32 off Interstate 94. The trail starts at the west end of the paved rim walkway, descends on wooden steps, and splits into a loop after 0.1 mile. It then descends through badlands, passes through a juniper grove, and then winds along a grassland before climbing back to the start. The views of the South Unit from Painted Canyon are among the park's finest.

SKYLINE VISTA TRAIL The *Skyline Vista Trail* (0.2 mile, South Unit) is a short walk from the Scenic Loop Drive (N46 56.104, W103 31.862) at 4.2 miles to an overlook above Interstate 94 and the Little Missouri River. The asphalt trail is handicapped accessible.

RIDGELINE NATURE TRAIL The *Ridgeline Nature Trail* (0.6 mile, South Unit) is a self-guided interpretive trail that begins at a pullout on the Scenic Loop Drive 10.8 miles from the Medora Visitor Center (N46 55.317, W103 27.788). It begins with a climb to a small butte top bench where the trail loop starts. The trail and interpretive guide explore a prairie environment, focusing on plant life and the effects of fire. There are some steep steps on the return. Bison use this trail and may lounge in the trailhead parking area. In May of 2019, part of the Scenic Loop Drive was closed due to erosion and slumping. The park has closed the road from near the start of the loop at 7.0 miles through the Badlands Overlook at 11.4 miles. The trail is still accessible to individuals who wish to hike or bike the road into the trailhead.

COAL VEIN NATURE TRAIL The *Coal Vein Nature Trail* (0.8 mile, South Unit) is an interpretive loop trail. It begins at the end of a 0.8-mile gravel road that leaves the Scenic Loop Drive 15.6 miles from the Medora Visitor Center (N46 55.467, W103 24.113). The loop explores an area where a seam of lignite coal burned underground from 1951 through 1977. If you ever wondered about the source of the red scoria used on so many of North Dakota's gravel roads, this is the place to find the answer. Part of the trail traverses outcroppings of bentonite clay, which is extremely slippery when wet.

BUCK HILL TRAIL The *Buck Hill Trail* (0.2 mile, South Unit) begins at the end of a 0.8-mile long gravel road that leaves the Scenic Loop Drive 17.1 miles from the Medora Visitor Center (N46 55.588, W103 23.374). The trail leads up an asphalt path to a sandstone topped hill and natural stone bench with a panoramic vista of the badlands above Paddock Creek. Visitors can enjoy spectacular views of the badlands surrounding Paddock Creek and the Painted Canyon Visitor Center perched on the prairie rim to the south.

BOICOURT OVERLOOK TRAIL The *Boicourt Overlook Trail* (0.4 mile, South Unit) was completed in 2005 and is a pleasant diversion for those driving the loop road. The trail starts at the overlook at mile point 19.9 on the Scenic Loop Drive. (N46 57.555, W103 24.093) The first 0.2 mile of the former game trail is now covered with gravel and is wheelchair accessible. The trail extends another 0.2 mile to an overlook at the top of a small butte (N46 57.337, W103 24.361). Informal routes continue to the south to descend to the Lower Talkington Trail.

WIND CANYON NATURE TRAIL The *Wind Canyon Nature Trail* (0.3 mile, South Unit) leads from the Scenic Loop Drive 25.1 miles from the Medora Visitor Center via the Scenic Loop Drive, or it may be accessed 4.0 miles on the main road after the start of the loop (N46 59.321, W103 29.084). The loop trail leads to an impressive overlook above the Little Missouri River. Wind Canyon's name comes from the unusual way the canyon was formed. Instead of having been carved primarily by water, the canyon is partly the result of erosion by wind as the prevailing westerly winds abrade the soft rock of the canyon sculpting the characteristic fluting of the walls. The overlooks along the trail are an excellent spot to watch the sunset and to look for herds of bison crossing the Little Missouri River below.

CCC TRAIL The *CCC Trail* (0.9 mile one way, South Unit) connects the Jones Creek trailhead parking area (N46 57.964, W103 29.266) with the Peaceful Valley trailhead (N46 57.546, W103 30.259). From the Peaceful Valley trailhead, the CCC Trail starts to the right from the signboard and goes east behind the Ranch's corral. The Ekblom Trail immediately splits left toward the Little Missouri River. Halfway through the trail is a typically wet creek crossing. Just before reaching the Scenic Loop Drive at the Jones Creek Trail, the CCC Trail passes an old well site with a concrete foundation.

The CCC Trail received heavy use from the park's saddle horse concession when it was operating, but currently is much less used.

MIKE AUNEY TRAIL The *Mike Auney Trail* (2.8 miles, South Unit) was opened in 1997 to provide trail access from the Roundup Horse Camp. It leads from the horse camp 1.1 miles west across the Little Missouri River and climbs another 1.7 miles to intersect the Maah Daah Hey Trail at a point 0.4 mile north of the junction with the South Petrified Forest (at 57.8 miles on the MDH). The access road for Roundup Horse Camp has a locked gate so that only those with reservations can access the trailhead. However, other visitors are welcome to park at the wide intersection of the gravel East River and Roundup Camp roads and walk the road to the trailhead. Parking at the intersection will add 0.9 mile each way to the hike.

JONES CREEK TRAIL The *Jones Creek Trail* spur leads from the Scenic Loop Drive at milepost 20.9 for 1.0 mile to a junction with the Lower Talkington Trail. Since the rest of Jones Creek most often is walked as a loop with the Lower Paddock Creek trail, this one-mile spur makes an excellent short stand-alone trip. From the end of the 0.1 mile gravel road to the trailhead (N46 58.112, W103 25.270), the trail leads about one hundred feet to a register box. After crossing a wet coulee, the trail follows the north bank of the creek to the Lower Talkington Trail junction (N46 58.029, W103 26.311).

MAAH DAAH HEY TRAIL The *Maah Daah Hey Trail (MDH)* traverses the South Unit from miles 52.5 to 60.7 on the west side of the Little Missouri River. Detailed descriptions of the Maah Daah Hey Trail are given in the Petrified Forest Loop and Lone Tree Loop trail descriptions in this chapter, and in the description of the Maah Daah Hey Trail from Sully Creek to Wannagan Campgrounds in the Maah Daah Hey Trail chapter. Keep in mind that it is no longer allowed to access the south end of the MDH in the South Unit at the ramp for Interstate 94 Exit 24. Vehicles parked here will be ticketed. The best way to reach the trail near Exit 24 is to take the paved Medora Bike Path from Chimney Park in Medora and hike 1.4 miles west to Exit 24. The Little Missouri National Grassland plans to construct a trailhead parking lot at Buffalo Gap Campground for horses, bikers, and hikers to provide additional access near the south end of the MDH Trail in the park. The Maah Daah Hey Trail is closed to mountain bikes in the National Park.

Miles 133.5 to 135.5 of the Maah Daah Hey Trail also cross the North Unit of Theodore Roosevelt National Park. This section crosses a designated Wilderness Area and is closed to mountain bikes. Since the trail does not connect to others in the North Unit, it is used primarily by those planning to hike or horseback ride long sections of the MDH. A detailed description of this trail is given in the description of the Maah Daah Hey Trail from Bennett Campground to the CCC Campground.

MEDORA BIKE PATH Though not a National Park Service trail, the *Medora Bike Path* is a handy 1.4 mile long connector between the town of Medora and the Maah Daah Hey Trail where it intersects the park boundary at the exit ramp for Exit 24, where parking is no longer permitted. You can access the paved bike path at the Chimney Park parking area on the west side of town, just west of the entry for Theodore Roosevelt National Park. The paved bike path crosses the Little Missouri River and follows the north side of the highway to the exit ramp where it intersects the Maah Daah Hey.

LITTLE MO NATURE TRAIL The *Little Mo Nature Trail* (1.1 miles, North Unit) is the only option for a short loop hike in the North Unit. It starts from the road to Juniper Campground opposite the parking area located by a private residence and just north of a picnic shelter. The trail interprets the geology, flora, and fauna of the badlands along the Little Missouri River. Brochures are available in a kiosk at the trailhead. Turn right at the first split in the trail between posts 2 and 3 to follow the loop counterclockwise. A shortcut between points 9 and 20 gives the option for a 0.7-mile wheelchair accessible inner loop. The outer dirt loop crosses a service road, intersects the Buckhorn Trail, and climbs a small butte before briefly rejoining the Buckhorn Trail on the service road and then rejoining the paved inner loop.

ABOVE Bison grazing along the Scenic Loop Road in the South Unit.

OTHER ADVENTURES IN THEODORE ROOSEVELT NATIONAL PARK

CANOEING THE LITTLE MISSOURI RIVER

For those lucky enough to catch the river at proper levels, a float trip on the Little Missouri can be one of the most memorable ways to experience Theodore Roosevelt National Park and the surrounding badlands. The Little Missouri is the only river designated as a state scenic river by North Dakota, and even a short river trip can yield a bounty of watchable wildlife and a personalized tour of the rugged badlands topography that lines the river corridor.

Catching the right season and the right year is critical. Ice on the river typically breaks up in April. Warmer temperatures and spring rains can combine to produce a float season in May or June. Predicting suitable flows is difficult. For example, in 2005 high water yielded a good season, but in the previous three springs water levels were too low for river travel. After spring runoff, low water levels will typically require far more boat dragging than floating. It is best to check water levels at the visitor center in advance of, and immediately before, your trip since water levels can change daily. River gauges are available online for Medora (https://waterdata.usgs.gov/nd/nwis/uv/?site_no=06336000&PARAmeter_cd=63158,00065,00060) and Watford City (https://water.weather.gov/ahps2/hydrograph.php?gage=wtfn8&wfo=bis).

Theodore Roosevelt National Park considers a water depth of 2.5 feet at Medora and flows of at least 700 cubic feet per second (cfs) the minimum for fair canoeing, with water depths of 2.5-3.5 feet and flows of 700-1500 cfs at Medora considered good to excellent.

When water levels are sufficient, a variety of both short and longer trips are possible. Floating from Sully Creek State Park to Medora (3 miles) or from Medora to Cottonwood Creek Campground (3.5 miles) can take about an hour for each section in high water, or can be half-day trips in the lower flows typical in most years. Another option for a short trip in the North Unit is from Juniper Campground to US 85 at the Long X Bridge (5.6 miles), which usually takes about two hours. Longer trip options include the section from Medora to Elkhorn Ranch (40 miles) and Elkhorn Ranch to US 85 (70 miles). The full 110 mile trip between the South and North Units typically requires three to four days. There are no designated launch facilities at any of these areas.

Planning for a float trip should consider the same food, water, clothing, weather protection, and map suggestions that apply to hikers in Theodore Roosevelt National Park. Specific items needed for the river are personal flotation devices (PFDs, or "life jackets" to us civilians), extra paddles, buckets for bailing, dry bags or plastic bags for protecting gear, and river shoes for those inevitable shallow spots where the boat must be dragged. Be prepared for portages that will be necessary where wildlife fences have been strung across the boundaries of the national park or between private lands. Some of these fences may be electrified.

Overnight trips on the Little Missouri are a rare treat, but they add to the complexity of trip planning with vehicle shuttles and the need to find camping areas. Boaters may be able to utilize the same shuttle services as those looking to bike long sections of the Maah Daah Hey Trail. Access to the river between the North and South units of Theodore Roosevelt National Park is more difficult than it appears on maps. If you are driving the maze of gravel roads in the Dakota Prairie Grasslands, remember that new roads may be built at any time and that road maintenance conditions can change. Roads, particularly those with any sort of grade, can quickly become impassable when wet.

ABOVE The Little Missouri Nature Trail in the North Unit.

Perhaps the best river access between the South and North units is at the Elkhorn Ranch Unit via DPG Road 2.

Riverside camping is allowed only on Dakota Prairie Grasslands or Theodore Roosevelt National Park lands. Most of the river bottom is privately held; use your map to stay on public land. If you camp on TRNP land, a free backcountry permit from a Visitor Center is needed. Using a camp stove and practicing Leave No Trace camping will ensure a better trip for your group and for others who follow. Finally, though motors are allowed on the river, their use is impractical due to shallow water and heavy silt.

THE PARK'S SCENIC DRIVES

For any visitor to a national park, a scenic drive is often the best option for getting an introduction to the area. For some visitors, their driving trip is often their only direct experience with the park. In Theodore Roosevelt, even visitors who may venture deep into the backcountry will appreciate the front country drive for the beauty of its scenery and for the unparalleled wildlife watching. If possible, take your trip near dusk or dawn, when the wildlife is most active and traffic is light. The light for photography is also at its best. The legendary mountain photographer Galen Rowell described early morning and late evening as the "magic hour" for the effect this light had on his pictures.

For road cyclists visiting Theodore Roosevelt National Park, or mountain bikers wishing to ride in the park, these scenic drives are your only options for biking. Mountain biking is not allowed on the trails in TRNP and the options for other road rides in the area are limited.

• **SOUTH UNIT SCENIC LOOP DRIVE** The *South Unit Scenic Loop Drive* is 36 miles roundtrip. The park sells "A Road Log Guide for the South and North Units" that serves as an excellent introduction to the geology of the park and it identifies the key features of the overlooks and nature trails found along the way. There are also six short nature trails along the loop that explore a variety of habitats and ecosystems and lead to some of the park's most impressive overlooks.

The Scenic Loop Drive begins at the Medora Visitor Center, passes the Cottonwood Campground and reaches the start of the loop at 6.6 miles. At 24.9 miles from the visitor center near the end of the loop, a spur leads north to Roundup Horse Camp, then north out of the park. The loop then passes Peaceful Valley and closes at 29.1 miles. Another 6.6 miles will return you to Medora. Short gravel side roads (0.8 mile each) lead to nature trails and overlooks at Coal Vein and Buck Hill at 15.6 and 17.1 miles, respectively. In May of 2019, part of the Scenic Loop Drive was closed due to erosion and slumping.

The park has closed the road from near the start of the loop at 7.0 miles through the Badlands Overlook at 11.4 miles. Due to the extent of the damage and the expected high cost of repair, there is currently no estimate for when the full loop may be reopened.

For me, the highlight of the Scenic Loop Drive is seeing the South Unit's herd of wild horses. There is no better symbol of the West than a wild stallion and his closely guarded herd roaming through the deep draws and steep hillsides of the badlands. These small bands of horses move frequently, so consider yourself lucky if you do observe them. Both bison and prairie dogs, two other icons of the West, are much easier to spot along the way. Mule deer, pronghorn, and elk are more likely to be seen near sunrise or sunset. Listen quietly and enjoy the sounds of birds chirping, prairie dogs yipping, and the bark of a distant coyote.

ABOVE Narrow-leaved bluebells.

- **NORTH UNIT SCENIC DRIVE** The *North Unit Scenic Drive* leads 13.7 miles from the Entrance Station near US 85 to a dead end near Oxbow Overlook, high above the Little Missouri River on the western edge of the park. The North Unit Visitor Center is located at 0.1 mile, and the turnoff to the Juniper Campground is at 4.6 miles. There are ten other pullouts along the way. The most spectacular of these is Riverbend Overlook and the magnificent stone shelter at 7.8 miles, built by the Civilian Conservation Corps in 1937. The overlook is the site of most of the calendar shots taken in the North Unit. The road closes in winter at the Caprock Coulee Nature Trail trailhead.

In 2019 the North Dakota Department of Transportation began upgrading US 85 to a four-lane highway from Watford to Belfield. These improvements will eventually include a surfaced trail from Watford City to the Little Missouri River alongside the newly widened highway.

ELKHORN RANCH UNIT

A visit to the Elkhorn Ranch Unit of Theodore Roosevelt National Park takes travelers through some of the most remote parts of the Little Missouri badlands. But this trip to the site of Roosevelt's primary residence is well worth the time and effort. No buildings remain at the site, but exhibits show the site of Roosevelt's house and other ranch structures. The site is still so quiet and remote one can imagine approaching the ranch to find the future president sitting on the shaded porch, serenaded by the rustle of wind through cottonwoods.

Ask at any visitor center for a copy of the map showing the ranch layout and access to it. You can reach Elkhorn Ranch using the directions for the Maah Daah Hey Trail Elkhorn Camp, which is 2.0 miles west of the ranch site. The park suggests driving westbound to exit 10, then turning right on gravel County Road 11 for 8.8 miles. Next, turn right on Westerheim Road for 6.5 miles. Then, turn left on Bell Lake Road for 11.7 miles. Finally, turn right onto DPG 2 towards the Maah Daah Hey Elkhorn Campground. Follow DPG 2 for 3.0 miles, continuing past the campground and trailhead to the Elkhorn Ranch Unit parking area.

Access to the ranch from the east side of the Little Missouri River is more difficult and requires fording the river. From the Scenic Loop Drive, drive north past Roundup Horse Camp out of TRNP to reach unpaved DPG Road 702. It is 22 miles from the Scenic Loop Drive to the junction with the Blacktail Road (DPG Road 2) and another 2.0 miles to the river, opposite the Elkhorn Ranch Site. Alternatively, this point can be reached from US 85 at the Fairfield town site by following the Black Tail Road (DPG 2) for 23 miles.

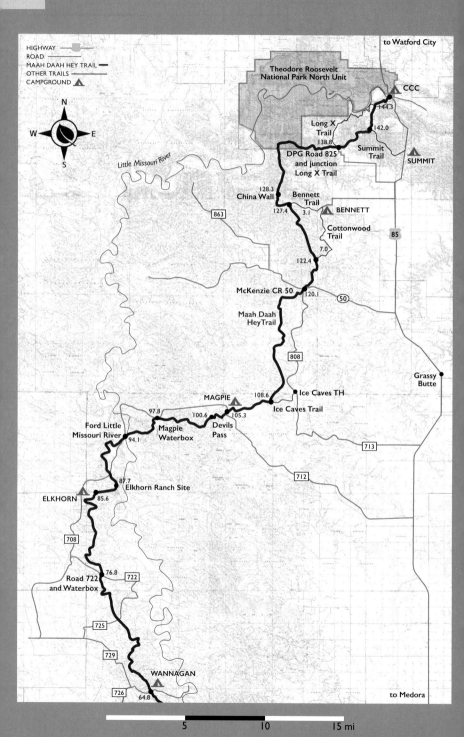

2

MAAH DAAH HEY NATIONAL RECREATION TRAIL

Hidden in a remote corner of western North Dakota is one of the country's most spectacular single-track trails. Here is the chance to ride rugged badlands, hike through scenic parks filled with wildlife, and enjoy it all without the crowds. It is because we have enjoyed this trail so much, and because of the growing interest in the recreation opportunities in the region, that this guidebook exists.

In 2003, the original Maah Daah Hey Trail was designated a National Recreation Trail, an honor that brings no extra funding or protection, but does bring higher national visibility to the trail. The entire 144 miles of the Maah Daah Hey Trail, including the new southern portion, was designated a National Recreation Trail on December 14, 2016.

The MDH connects the North and South units of Theodore Roosevelt National Park through the badlands and grasslands of the Little Missouri National Grassland. The trail was originally conceived by horseback riders seeking a long, challenging route across the badlands, but the trail is also open to hikers. Mountain bikers, who may now be the most frequent trail users, can ride the trail except in the two units of Theodore Roosevelt National Park, where the route crosses two designated wilderness areas. The Buffalo Gap Trail bypasses the park's South Unit, but there is currently no formal bypass route for bikers around the North Unit. The trail is managed as a cooperative effort between North Dakota Parks and Recreation, Theodore Roosevelt National Park (TRNP), and the Dakota Prairie

ABOVE The Maah Daah Hey Trail near Coal Creek Campground.

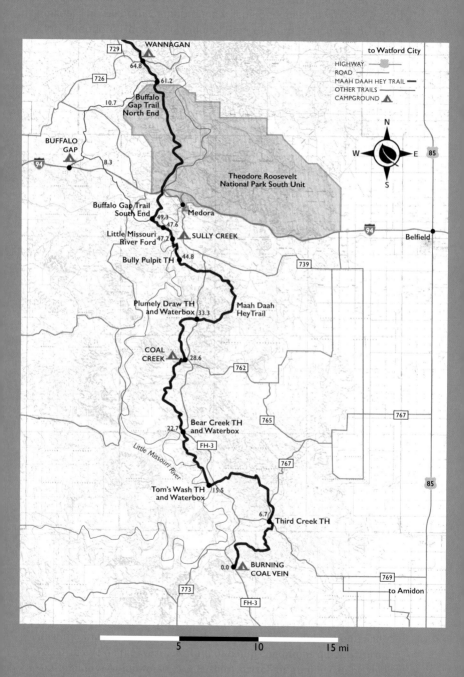

Grasslands (DPG) of the United States Forest Service.

Almost immediately after the construction of the initial 96 miles of the Maah Daah Hey Trail between Sully Creek and the CCC Campground, the LMNG made plans to extend the trail to the south at the request of the Slope County Commissioners. The new trail was variously called the Maah Daah Hey II, or less formerly the Deuce, but the LMNG now prefers the less confusing designation as the southern portion of the MDH. A trail route was designed that would extend south from Sully Creek to Amidon, near the southern limit of contiguous Forest Service controlled land and White Butte, the highest point in North Dakota. Due to management and right-of-way concerns, the route was shortened to just go to Burning Coal Vein Campground.

Work on the southern portion began in 2007 with the drilling of a water well at Burning Coal Vein Campground. By 2011, most of the north and south section ends of the trail were in place. The southern portion was officially opened in June 2014, though a gap between the Bully Pulpit trailhead and Sully Creek Campground existed where there was no public land to locate the trail. In 2015, that gap was closed and the Maah Daah Hey reached its current 144.3 continuous miles. Moving MP 0 at the start of the trail from Sully Creek to Burning Coal Vein made it necessary to change the rest of the mileposts along the trail and this was done in 2016. The first edition of this guide was published in 2006, before the building of the southern portion of the MDH, and the inclusion of the new trail is the most important and exciting change between the first and second editions.

The original Maah Daah Hey Trail was built with hikers and horseback riders as the expected users, but the lure of one hundred miles of singletrack quickly pulled in far more mountain bikers, which the Maah Daah Hey Trail Association estimates to be 70% of all trail users. The trail is ideal for experienced riders. The combination of wild landforms and wide-open spaces is unmatched by any other biking trail. It has a good mix of challenging, technical singletrack across the rugged badlands and easy cruising along the flat, grassy tablelands. Their greater range gives mountain bikers fewer water problems than long-distance hikers or horseback riders. By the time the southern portion was designed and constructed, the trail could be built with bike riders in mind. Most riders agree that the southern portion has better flow for biking and is a bit easier riding due to the improved trail design. The DPG is continuing to enhance and maintain the trail with projects such as hardening the trail surface with gravel to provide an all-weather route and prevent erosion and rutting of the trail by both bikes and livestock.

Though the Little Missouri badlands are not as isolated as they were in Theodore Roosevelt's time, the scenery remains every bit as captivating. Much of the trail passes through well-developed badlands landscapes, where bizarre landforms vie with petrified wood and eye-grabbing vistas for the traveler's attention. Wildlife watchers will enjoy frequent sightings of pronghorn along with the opportunity to spot bison, elk, bighorn sheep, and wild turkey. The route is remote enough that it is possible to spend all day on the trail and not see other people.

The name Maah Daah Hey and the trail's turtle symbol come from the Mandan Indians. *Maah Daah Hey* means an area that "has been or will be" around for a long time. The turtle is a symbol of determination, steadfastness, patience, and fortitude, and is a way to honor ancestors. The theme of longevity and permanence are ideal for a trail through a landscape unaltered by settlement of the West and leading through a national park dedicated to preserving Roosevelt's conservation legacy.

ABOVE Shadow of a mountain biker resting on the Maah Daah Hey Trail.

The trail is marked with tall 4" x 6" wooden posts branded with the turtle emblem, though to many cynics the emblem resembles a tick. Mileposts mark the entire length of the trail. Though a few short sections of trail follow older two-track dirt roads, most of the trail in the Dakota Prairie Grasslands was built as new singletrack, while existing routes were used in Theodore Roosevelt National Park. Generally, the trail is well-worn and easy to follow, though it is possible to get misled by cattle or bison paths that cross the trail. Much of the trail is subject to grazing by livestock in the national grassland and bison in the national park. Both can disguise the MDH by beating in their own trails. Traffic from cattle can also damage the trail in wet conditions, leaving behind an obstacle course of sharp, deep hoof prints.

For mountain bike riders, the condition of the trail is a critical factor in how enjoyable a ride is. For Maah Daah Hey riders, two factors will control this. The first is how dry the trail is. Like all trails, it should not be ridden when wet. The MDH especially can be impassable when wet. Many stretches of trail have gumbo, which is an expandable clay that is extremely slippery, yet also has the ability to stick to almost anything, especially shoe soles and the tires of bikes. Also, as mentioned above, much of the Maah Daah Hey Trail in the national grassland passes through areas with active cattle grazing. Riders can generally avoid cattle and their droppings, but occasionally cattle are released into plots crossed by the trail when the ground is still wet. This can lead to extensive pocking of the trail surface and can, at its extreme, also make the trail unrideable. Unfortunately, while it is easy to determine early in a ride if the trail is too wet, damage of the trail by cattle is unpredictable. I last rode the southern portion in the very wet year of 2019, and while some short sections were damaged by cattle, none of these sections were long and all were still ridable.

The Dakota Prairie Grasslands constructed five campgrounds at Coal Creek, Wannagan, Elkhorn, Magpie, and Bennett, each about 20 miles apart along the trail to go along with the two previously existing campgrounds at Burning Coal Vein and CCC that anchor the south and north ends of the trail. These fenced campgrounds offer vault toilets, campsites with fire rings and picnic tables, and most importantly, water wells. The wells are operated by hand pumps, with the exception of Coal Creek which is solar-powered. The pumps are turned on during the summer season and normally run from around May through December. Please check with the DPG to ensure the pumps are working before you start your trip. Four of the five camps are on short side trails off the Maah Daah Hey Trail. However, Bennett Camp is located three miles from the main trail. The DPG Buffalo Gap and Summit campgrounds are located at the trailheads for their namesake connector trails. Sully Creek State Park at 47.2 miles, just south of Medora, has a full-service campground that includes pay showers. The Cottonwood Campground in the South Unit of Theodore Roosevelt National Park is located close to, but across the Little Missouri River from, the trail at 54.6 miles.

Backcountry camping is permitted anywhere on the Dakota Prairie Grasslands. However, private and state-owned sections of the Maah Daah Hey Trail are off-limits to camping and travelers are confined to the trail in these sections. Those planning to stay in either unit of Theodore Roosevelt National Park must obtain a free backcountry permit.

The Maah Daah Hey Trail crosses both units of Theodore Roosevelt National Park. Besides the protection that these areas receive as part of the national park, most of the North Unit and much of the South Unit west of the Little Missouri River are further protected as part of the Theodore Roosevelt Wilderness Area. Designation as wilderness areas means that mechanized vehicles, including mountain bikes, are prohibited. Though this designation does not affect hikers or horseback riders using the trail, it creates problems for mountain bikers. To give bikers a route around the park's South Unit, the DPG has constructed the 19-mile Buffalo Gap Trail, which bypasses the Maah Daah Hey Trail from just north of the Sully Creek Campground to the grassland north of the South Unit of TRNP, and also connects to the DPG Buffalo Gap Campground.

Like much of the Little Missouri National Grassland, the land around the North Unit of Theodore Roosevelt National Park is a patchwork of Forest Service, state, and private land. In this case, however, there is no continuous corridor of public land where a bypass trail could be built. With no option to connect the trail across the North Unit, bikers often start their journeys south from the Bennett Campground on the Cottonwood or Bennett trails, skipping the first 17 miles of the Maah Daah Hey Trail.

Though the Maah Daah Hey Trail was designed and built as a point-to-point trail, most trail users prefer loop routes for their one-day trips. After all, why ride the same trail twice when you could be covering new ground all day long? Thanks to the construction of side trails there are several possible loops using the MDH, plus a few other options for those who don't mind riding a bit of gravel road. Hikers and horseback riders have the option of combining the Buffalo Gap and Maah Daah Hey trails for a 31-mile loop. Those who don't mind a bit of riding or hiking on roads with low traffic can combine the Maah Daah Hey and Ice Caves trails with ten miles of DPG roads 808 and 809 for a 21-mile loop. The Cottonwood and Bennett trails can be combined with the MDH for a 15.1-mile loop. Finally, the Long X Trail can be combined

with the last five miles of the Maah Daah Hey Trail for an 11.3-mile loop.
Two sections of the new southern portion, Plumely to Bully Pulpit and
Burning Coal Vein to Toms Wash are also easy to make into loops by
riding short sections of the well-maintained gravel access county roads.
Finally, commercial shuttles provided by Dakota Cyclery in Medora
are a popular and easy way to ride the Maah Daah Hey. The rides
into Medora from Plumely trailhead, Buffalo Gap Campground, and
Wannagan Campground are the most popular shuttle trips.

When shuttles or loops are not practical, many groups will base
themselves out of the trail campgrounds and do out and back hikes
north and south along the trail. Travelers are often surprised out how
different the badlands vistas can be from heading different directions
on the same trail.

While often very scenic, the DPG segments of the Maah Daah Hey
Trail do not offer the wilderness experience found in TRNP. Parts of
the trail pass through active oil and gas fields. Trail users should give
well facilities a wide berth due to hazards from poisonous gasses. The
other main use of the grasslands is cattle grazing, an activity popular
since Roosevelt's time. The signs of cattle will be all around you.
Their paths may obscure the official trail, and their muddy hoof prints
can make rough riding. However, it is important to realize that the
grassland is a multiple-use area. It is the energy firms and the counties
that maintain most of the access roads under permit or easements, and

ABOVE Views from the Maah Daah Hey Trail.

it is the cattle ranchers that maintain the stock tanks and dams.

Long distance travelers on the Maah Daah Hey Trail will face two main obstacles. The first challenges are two fords of the Little Missouri River, one in Sully Creek State Park near MP 47 and the other north of Elkhorn Ranch near MP 94, that roughly divide the trail into thirds. In many years, the river can be easily forded on hard bottom by late spring. However, in very wet years the river may be impassable, except by boat late, into the summer. It is wise to check on river levels with either the DPG or TRNP if you are planning a trip that requires a river crossing. Perversely, the long-distance traveler's other obstacle is lack of drinking water. However, since the first backpacking trips my wife and I took on the MDH in the early 2000s, access to water has much improved. In season, all the DPG campgrounds have potable water, as does the state park campground at Sully Creek. To fill in the gaps between campgrounds, the DPG now provides eight waterboxes, donated by the Maah Daah Hey Trail Association, where water can be cached. The metal boxes are located just off the trail, where they are not visible from the road but still easily reached. Their locations are

ABOVE Waterboxes are located along the trail to enable users to cache water.

marked by a blue dot in the center of the Maah Daah Hey turtle marker. All are located at trailheads or off well-maintained gravel county roads.

Waterbox users should label their cache containers with their name and date. Do not leave food, garbage, or any other items in the cache. Occasionally there will be donated water in the caches, but do not count on getting water from the waterboxes unless you have put it there yourself. If you set up a cache, remember your Leave No Trace practices and haul out everything that you've carried in.

The eight waterbox locations are below:

TABLE 2 - WATERBOXES

Third Creek Trailhead	Mile 6.7
Toms Wash Trailhead	Mile 15.5
Bear Creek Trailhead	Mile 22.7
Plumely Draw Trailhead	Mile 33.2
Roosevelt DPG 722 Junction	Mile 76.8
Magpie Road DPG 712 Junction	Mile 97.8
Beicegal Creek Road DPG 809 Junction	Mile 119.2
Long X Trail Junction, DPG 825 Junction	Mile 138.8

Outside of the campgrounds and waterboxes, it is difficult to find water of good enough quality to be treatable. The Maah Daah Hey Trail crosses some major creeks large enough to hold water into the summer, but these creeks are unreliable. Other options are the year-round springs and seasonal stock ponds and tanks in the DPG used to water cattle in summer. The DPG's MDH trail map shows the locations of the year-round flowing wells and springs. This water is often unappetizing in appearance and could be undrinkable after the cattle are brought from their winter pastures to the grasslands. If you are forced to rely on this water, look for the intake pipe to the stock tanks; it may be possible to get fresher water here. Remember that any water you find along the trail must be treated before drinking.

To cover the entire length of the Maah Daah Hey Trail, most groups will need to arrange a shuttle from one end to the other. Dakota Cyclery in Medora offers a variety of shuttle services ranging from day trips on the MDH and Buffalo Gap trails, to fully supported end-to-end trips. Backpackers looking to cover the MDH in three trips could use the strategy my wife and I followed to complete the trail. For the north third of the trail, we left our vehicle at the CCC Campground and were shuttled to County Road 712. After a quick side trip to the Little Missouri River we hiked to the north end of the trail. For the middle third, we were shuttled to DPG Road 708 then again walked back to our vehicle, after taking a side trip to the river. The southern third of the southern portion can be done with an easy shuttle via DPG 3. This approach eliminates the need for the middle ford of the Little Missouri River.

Severe wind and cold during winter and the hot, dry heat of summer will likely ensure that the Maah Daah Hey Trail receives more use in the spring and fall. Be prepared for extremes of temperature, sun, and wind at any time of year. There are also many stretches of trail across gumbo, a remarkably sticky and heavy type of clay that is impassable when wet. It is better to wait a few hours for the trail to dry than to attempt to ride it when wet. The western Dakotas are one of the country's least populated regions making cell phone reception very rare, so keep in mind that you're on your own in these badlands.

Two organizations have been formed to support the Maah Daah Hey Trail and could use your support. The Maah Daah Hey Trail Association (mdhta.com) was formed in 2000 to promote and help maintain the MDH trail system in conjunction with the Forest Service and the other partners. It provides the most up-to-date information on the current conditions and status of the trail. The group's website has an excellent interactive map of the trail and contains GPX files of the MDH and its connecting trails for upload to GPS devices. Their Turtle Tracks newsletter also contains the latest trail-related information.

Save the Maah Daah Hey is a nonprofit organization that works in partnership with the Forest Service to maintain the MDH and has donated thousands of hours of volunteer labor to the cause. The group was started in 2013 by Nick Ybarra partly in response to the maintenance backlog on the trail caused by the extremely wet spring of 2013. Ybarra also organizes the MDH 100 and associated mountain bike and running races. The group can be reached on Facebook or through the website for Ybarra's race events (www.experienceland.org).

TABLE 3 - MAAH DAAH HEY TRAIL MILEAGE

	TOTAL MILEAGE	INTERVAL DISTANCE	SECTION DISTANCE
Burning Coal Vein Trailhead DPG Road 772	0.0	0	0.0
Cross DPG Road 772	0.3	0.3	0.3
Third Creek Trailhead & Waterbox DPG Road 769	6.7	6.4	6.7
Cross DPG Road 767	8.5	1.8	8.5
Hanleys Wash Bridge	9.5	1.0	9.5
Toms Wash Trailhead & Waterbox FS 3	15.5	6.0	15.5
Cross Bridge over Toms Wash	16.0	0.5	0.5
Vista	17.5	1.5	2.0
Cross DPG Road 746	21.4	3.9	5.9
Bear Creek TH FS 3 & Waterbox (0.3 mile east)	22.7	1.3	7.2
Cross Dantz Creek	26.0	3.3	10.5
Cross DPG Road 794	26.9	0.9	11.4
Cross Tepee Creek	27.2	0.3	11.7
Coal Creek CG (0.7 mile east)	28.6	1.4	13.1
Cross Merrifield Creek	30.0	1.4	14.5
Cross Little Creek	32.0	2.0	16.5
Plumely Draw TH & Waterbox FS 3	33.3	1.3	17.8
Trail Post Butte	35.0	1.7	1.7
Grasslands Gate	37.1	2.1	3.8
Davis Creek	38.5	1.4	5.2
Ridgetop Gate	40.0	1.4	6.7
Narrow Badlands Gate	41.6	1.6	8.3
Cross FH 3	42.7	1.1	9.4
Cross DPG Road 742-2	44.0	1.3	10.7
Bully Pulpit TH & Bully Pulpit Jct	44.8	0.8	11.5
Sully Creek State Park TH	47.2	2.4	13.9

TABLE 3 - MAAH DAAH HEY TRAIL MILEAGE

	TOTAL MILEAGE	INTERVAL DISTANCE	SECTION DISTANCE
Little Missouri River Ford	47.6	0.4	0.4
Buffalo Gap Trail, South End	49.3	1.7	2.1
Andrews Creek	52.1	2.8	4.9
Medora Bike Path and Enter TRNP	52.5	0.4	5.3
Cottonwood Register Box	54.6	2.1	7.4
Ekblom Trail Junction	55.6	1.0	8.4
Lone Tree Spring Loop Trail	56.0	0.4	8.8
Big Plateau Trail Junction	57.2	1.2	10.0
South Petrified Forest Trail Junction	57.4	0.2	10.2
Mike Auney Trail Junction	57.8	0.4	10.6
North Petrified Forest Trail Junction	60.7	2.9	13.5
Buffalo Gap Trail, North End	61.2	0.5	14.0
Cross DPG Road 726	64.5	3.3	17.3
Wannagan Camp (0.2 mile west)	64.8	0.3	17.6
Cross DPG Road 728	67.8	3.0	3.0
Crooked Creek	71.4	3.6	6.6
Cross DPG Road 725	72.4	1.0	7.6
Roosevelt Creek	75.0	2.6	10.2
Cross DPG Road 722 & Waterbox	76.8	1.8	12.0
Dry Creek	81.2	4.4	16.4
Ellison Creek	83.3	2.1	18.5
Elkhorn Camp (0.3 mile west)	85.6	2.3	20.8
Elkhorn Trailhead FH 2	86.0	0.4	0.4
TRNP Elkhorn Ranch Site	87.7	1.7	2.1
South Crossing DPG Road 708	89.1	1.4	3.5
North Crossing DPG Road 708	93.1	4.0	7.5

TABLE 3 - MAAH DAAH HEY TRAIL MILEAGE

	TOTAL MILEAGE	INTERVAL DISTANCE	SECTION DISTANCE
Ford Little Missouri River	94.1	1.0	8.5
DPG Road 712	97.4	3.3	11.8
Magpie Waterbox	97.8	0.4	12.2
Devils Pass	100.6	2.8	15.0
Pond	101.5	0.9	15.9
Cross DPG Road 711	102.2	0.7	16.6
Cross FS 712 at Magpie TH	105.2	3.0	19.6
Magpie Camp (0.3 mile north)	105.3	0.1	19.7
Cross Magpie Creek	105.6	0.3	0.3
Ice Caves Trail Junction	108.6	3.0	3.3
DPG Road 809 and Pond	114.9	6.3	9.6
Beicegal Creek	115.4	0.5	10.1
DPG Road 809 & Beicegal Waterbox	119.2	3.8	13.9
McKenzie County Road 50	120.1	0.9	14.8
Cottonwood Trail (7.0 miles to Bennett Trailhead)	122.4	2.3	17.1
West Fork Cottonwood Creek	124.0	1.6	18.7
Bennett Trail Junction (campground is 3.1 miles east)	127.4	3.4	22.1
China Wall	128.3	0.9	0.9
DPG Road 823 near Bennett Creek	130.0	1.7	2.6
Pond at Collar Draw	132.4	2.4	5.0
Enter TRNP North Unit	133.6	1.2	6.2
Leave TRNP North Unit	135.4	1.8	8.0
DPG Road 825 and Junction Long X Trail	138.8	3.4	11.4
Summit Trail	142.0	3.2	14.6
CCC Trail Junction	144.0	2.0	16.6
CCC Campground	144.3	0.3	16.9

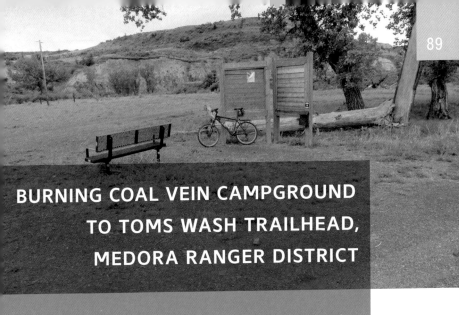

BURNING COAL VEIN CAMPGROUND TO TOMS WASH TRAILHEAD, MEDORA RANGER DISTRICT

Remote singletrack trail at the south end of the Maah Daah Hey.

GENERAL LOCATION: Twenty-three miles south of Medora, North Dakota.

HIGHLIGHT: Ridgetop riding and views of the badlands.

ACCESS: From Medora, turn south from Pacific Avenue onto East River Road South (DPG 3). Drive south past the Toms Wash trailhead, which is the north end of the ride at 21.3 miles. Continue south to a signed junction with DPG 772 at 27.3 miles. Turn left and follow DPG 772 for 1.3 miles into the Burning Coal Vein Campground and bear right at a fork in the campground to reach the Maah Daah Hey trailhead (N46 35.896, W103 26.696). The gravel roads are well maintained and suitable for passenger cars. If the length of your trip dictates caching water, you can utilize the water boxes at Third Creek, Toms Wash, Bear Creek, or Plumley Draw, as well as get water at the solar pump at Coal Creek Campground, all of which are easily accessible off DPG 3. The Burning Coal Vein Campground has eight sites, some shade, a latrine, and a seasonal pump for water.

DISTANCE: This segment is 15.5 miles one-way.

ALLOWED USES: This trail is open to all non-motorized users, including hikers, mountain bikers, and horseback riders.

LEFT The adventure begins: the southern end of the Maah Daah Hey Trail.
ABOVE The Third Creek Trailhead.

MAPS: Little Missouri National Grassland Maah Daah Hey National Recreation Trail 2018, Maah Daah Hey Trail Association Trail Guide (mdhta.com/trail-guide), Trails Illustrated Theodore Roosevelt National Park (#259), and USGS Juniper Spur and Cliffs Plateau, ND 7.5-minute quadrangles, and Map D.

Toms Wash and the Burning Coal Vein Campground are 15 miles apart by trail, but only seven miles apart by road, making for an enticing loop option for those riders who don't mind grinding a little gravel. The opportunity to camp at Burning Coal Vein Campground with water and shaded campsites adds to the appeal of this section.

The Maah Daah Hey (MDH) Trail begins modestly by a gravel pullout, trail register, and nearly barren signboard. Start by going through a self-closing gate through a fence line. The cleverly designed gate is used throughout the trail and can easily be lifted and replaced to allow hikers and riders to quickly pass through the numerous fences that divide the pastures crossed by the MDH. Like all of the southern portion of the Maah Daah Hey Trail, this section has a well-defined tread and is marked with the large wooden posts branded with the distinctive Maah Daah Hey turtle symbol. Much of the trail is "surfaced" with 4-inch compacted depth of gravel that provides superior traction and a traversable trail surface in wet conditions. However, like all sections of the MDH, this one passes through rugged badlands and over gumbo areas, that super slippery/sticky clay that can make trails impassable when wet.

In 0.3 mile the Maah Daah Hey Trail crosses DPG 772, the campground road, then crosses another self-closing gate and a long wooden bridge over Second Creek. Weave through the grassland below a chain of badlands buttes. At 1.0 mile, reach MP 1, the first of many mile posts ahead. If you're planning to hike or ride the entire Maah Daah Hey, its one down and 143 to go! Next, traverse a narrow ridge at the head of some steep ravines, then ascend some switchbacks to reach the uppermost grassland. Enjoy some sweeping views from the grassland before a self-closing gate at 2.5 miles marks the start of a short descent.

At 4.6 miles, cross another gate with a power line adjacent to it that marks the start of a long gradual descent toward Third Creek. Just before MP 6, climb up and over a small ridge. Cross a gate and pass a waterbox before reaching the Third Creek trailhead at 6.7 miles (N47 37.816, W103 23.837) and DPG 769. The trailhead offers the first shade of the trip beneath some giant cottonwoods, a gravel parking area, trail register, signboard, and bench.

After your well-deserved break, turn left on DPG 769 to cross over Third Creek, then turn right off the road and up the nose of a small ridge. The trail next swings around the east side of a chain of badlands buttes before crossing DPG 767 at 8.5 miles (N47 39.031, W103 24.138) at another gate. MP 9 is located in a small grove of welcome trees above the head of a pond now filled with reeds. Reach a bridged crossing of signed Hanleys Wash at 9.5 miles (N47 39.701, W103 24.226). Hanleys is a particularly deep wash even for the badlands, so send some good vibes toward the trail builders of the Little Missouri National Grassland as you roll smoothly over it.

From the wash, the trail next climbs to Hanleys Plateau. MP 10 is found in the midst of some badlands switchbacks where the first petrified tree stumps of the MDH are found. From the plateau, enjoy the distant grasslands views and the blazingly fast downhill riding. After MP 12, begin a short, steady climb and reach a gate at 12.5 miles. A short section of badlands beyond has some petrified wood fragments. The next gate is located at 14.6 miles. Finish the ride with a long gradual descent to a gate at DPG 3 and the Toms Wash trailhead (N47 39.969, W103 28.581) at 15.5 miles.

The Toms Wash trailhead has minimal facilities: a gravel parking area, signboard, bench, and a waterbox are located just north on the trail.

ABOVE Beautiful singletrack north of Hanleys Wash.

TOMS WASH TRAILHEAD TO PLUMELY DRAW TRAILHEAD, MEDORA RANGER DISTRICT

Gentle riding across prairie and badlands.

GENERAL LOCATION: Seventeen miles south of Medora, North Dakota.

HIGHLIGHT: Fun riding with spectacular views of the Little Missouri River.

ACCESS: From Medora, turn south from Pacific Avenue onto East River Road South DPG 3). Drive south past the Plumely Draw trailhead, which is the north end of the ride at 8.3 miles. Continue south past the Coal Creek Campground at 11.5 miles and the Bear Creek trailhead at 15.9 miles to reach the Toms Wash trailhead at 21.3 miles (N47 39.969, W103 28.581). The Toms Wash trailhead has minimal facilities: a gravel parking area, signboard, bench, and a waterbox are located just north on the trail. The Bear Creek (0.3 mile) and Coal Creek (0.7 mile) trails connect to the Maah Daah Hey Trail from their trailheads. The gravel roads are well-maintained and suitable for passenger cars. If the length of your trip dictates caching water, you can utilize the water boxes at Bear Creek and Plumley Draw, as well as get water at the solar pump at Coal Creek Campground. The Coal Creek Campground has eight sites, some shade, a latrine, and a solar pump for water.

DISTANCE: This segment is 17.8 miles one-way.

ALLOWED USES: This trail is open to all non-motorized users, including hikers, mountain bikers, and horseback riders.

LEFT A grassland section of the Maah Daah Hey Trail.
ABOVE Scenic badlands near Bear Creek.

MAPS: Little Missouri National Grassland Maah Daah Hey
National Recreation Trail 2018, Maah Daah Hey Trail Association
Trail Guide (mdhta.com/trail-guide), Trails Illustrated Theodore
Roosevelt National Park (#259), and USGS Cliffs Plateau, Bullion
Butte, and Chimney Butte, ND 7.5-minute quadrangles, and Map D.

The middle of the southern portion of the Maah Daah Hey Trail
parallels well-graded DPG Forest Road 3 and passes by the Bear Creek
trailhead and another trailhead at the Coal Creek Campground. This
easy access means that riders have lots of options for picking their
route. However, the short sections between these access points can
easily be combined into a single day's ride that would be suitable for
beginning riders. Though this segment lacks the prolific wildlife found
in the National Park, pronghorn antelope are commonly seen.

This section traverses a mix of badlands topography and rolling
grasslands. The badlands here are not as extensive or as deeply incised
as badlands in the National Park to the north, or even along the
original Maah Daah Hey Trail between the two units. However, the
mix of badlands and grasslands makes for diverse riding and perhaps
even better long-distance views. While the original Maah Daah Hey
Trail was designed primarily with horseback riders and hikers in mind,
by the time this southern portion of the MDH was approved, mountain
bikers were already an important user of the trail. Consequently, riders
will find that much of the southern portion has a better flow for riding
than much of the original Maah Daah Hey. This section has an easy to
follow tread, and is well-signed with the tall, wooden MDH trail posts.

From the Toms Wash trailhead (mile 15.5), the Little Missouri
River is barely visible off to the west. A waterbox is located just west
of the trailhead, in view of the trailhead but not in view from DPG
3. From the trailhead, descend gently down to a bridged crossing of
signed Toms Wash shortly before reaching MP 16. The corresponding
climb out of the wash is gentle, but long. Cross a two-track ranch road
before reaching a line of bluffs above the river at MP 17.

Just beyond MP 17 are some of the best views of the Little
Missouri River found anywhere along the trail. Far below, the river
has cut the steep bluff topped by the trail, while the far side of the
river holds a broad meander encircling a large gravel bar. A hilltop
and self-closing gate near the north end of the bluff offer the best
viewing. Once past the bluffs, descend to a self-closing gate at 18.4
miles. Pass through a shady grove of juniper before reaching a short
wooden bridge over an unnamed creek at 19.6 miles. After MP 20,
climb sharply through a short section of badlands. Just beyond is an

impressive badlands vista. These last few miles south of Bear Creek are mostly gentle riding through rolling grasslands. At 21.4 miles, cross gravel DPG 746 (N46.42.945, W103 31.338) and wrap around the head of Bear Creek as the trail skirts the edge of DPG 3. After MP 22, climb gently to a waterbox and the junction with the Bear Creek Trail (N47 43.740, W103 31.288) at 22.7 miles, which leads right 0.3 mile to the Bear Creek trailhead (N47 43.628, W103 31.158) on DPG 3. The Bear Creek trailhead has a gravel parking area, signboard, register box, and bench.

From the Bear Creek junction, soon cross a self-closing gate then climb on switchbacks to a plateau rim marked by MP 23 and then cross a well-graded gravel road. The trail follows a long ridgeline to the northwest with views of Bullion Butte to the south southwest before starting to drop toward Dantz Creek. The start of the descent utilizes a few switchbacks, but the entire descent is relatively gentle. Just beyond MP 25 is the bridged crossing of a tributary by a self-closing gate. Next, reach the signed and bridged crossing of Dantz Creek (N46 45.382, W103 32.329) by a large, shady cottonwood tree just short of MP 26.

From Dantz Creek, climb up onto another flat prairie, crossing an old two-track road and self-closing gate along the way. At 26.9 miles, cross gravel DPG 794 (N46 44.887, W103 31.841), then descend into a lush grove of trees in the valley of Tepee Creek at 27.2 miles (N46 46.060, W103 31.901). Tepee Creek lacks enough water flow to carve a distinct channel for the creek.

Climb out of the valley of Tepee Creek via a modest badlands saddle. After MP 28, two old two-track roads will split off to the right on the top rolling grassland section. Next, descend into the valley of Coal Creek to reach a junction at 28.6 miles (N46 46.270, W103 31.485) with the Coal Creek Trail which leads 0.7 mile east to its namesake trailhead and campground.

To reach the campground, turn right onto the Coal Creek Trail and follow it along the north side of a tributary of the creek. At 0.6 mile, the unlabeled Survey Monument Trail (LMNG #7020) side trail leads left to a "Point of Interest" in 0.15 miles. The monument commemorates 100 years of the US Forest Service and is a survey control station calibrated by GPS for horizontal and vertical survey control. It is also used as a geocache site. Just beyond, the trail splits (N46 46.708, W103 30.947) with the left side reaching the trailhead in 0.1 mile and the right side reaching the campground in the same distance. The trailhead (N46 46.690, W103 30.868) has a gravel parking area, latrine, and signboard. The campground (N46 46.620, W103 30.909) was constructed in 2014 and offers ten sites with a solar-powered water well.

To continue north on the Maah Daah Trail from the Coal Creek junction, bear left to climb from the valley of Coal Creek. You'll see lots of clinker here, named for the distinctive sound the rock makes as you travel over it. Clinker is the bright red remains of shale fused together by the burning of underlying coal beds. Make a winding descent through open prairie to signed and bridged Merrifield Creek (N46 47.557, W103 31.394) just past MP 30.

Theodore Roosevelt met Bill Merrifield and his partner Sylvane Ferris early in his first trip to badlands in 1883. Roosevelt needed to borrow a horse for his buffalo hunting trip. The two experienced men understandably were reluctant to help, but finally agreed to provide a mount for Roosevelt. It was during this first hunting trip that Roosevelt began to plan his entry into the North Dakota cattle business. He eventually bought the herd of 150 head that Merrifield and Ferris had been herding and the ranch that went with them, the Maltese Cross. Merrifield and Ferris were hired to run the ranch and built the Maltese Cross Cabin during the winter of 1883-1884. After acquiring the Elkhorn Ranch, Roosevelt moved his headquarters to the new site, but continued to be active with Merrifield and Ferris at the Maltese Cross. Merrifield and Ferris grew the operation until the disastrous winter of 1886-87, when 80% of the region's cattle perished in the extreme cold and deep snow, and Roosevelt had lost over half his herd. Merrifield and Ferris tended to the remainder of Roosevelt's cattle after the Elkhorn Ranch closed in 1887, and the two men worked together until Merrifield quit in 1892.

The Merrifield Creek crossing marks the start of a switchbacked climb through badlands. At the top, pass a small corral and a self-closing gate where the trail nears DPG 3. The remainder of the trail to Plumely Draw traverses rolling grasslands where the wildflowers include textile onion, yellow asters, salsify, large yellow daisy, white penstemon, creeping juniper, and flea bane. Enjoy a few gentle switchbacks, then the trail crosses signed Little Creek (N46 48.842, W103 31.447) immediately beyond MP 32. At 33.2 miles the Plumely waterbox is on the right side of the trail. Reach the end of the segment at 33.3 miles at the Plumely Draw trailhead (N46 49.011, W103 30.334). The trailhead has a gravel parking area, signboard, trail register, and bench.

RIGHT "Maah Daah Hey" comes from the Mandan Hidatsa Indians and means "Grandfather" or "an area that has been or will be around for a long time." The trail system uses a turtle image on trail markers.

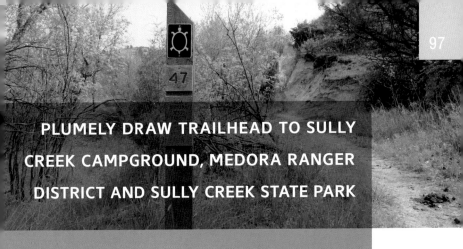

PLUMELY DRAW TRAILHEAD TO SULLY CREEK CAMPGROUND, MEDORA RANGER DISTRICT AND SULLY CREEK STATE PARK

An easily accessible section of the Maah Daah Hey Trail with a good mix of badlands and grasslands riding.

GENERAL LOCATION: Four miles south of Medora, ND.

HIGHLIGHT: A fast and scenic descent along the north half of the trail. The 2.5-mile hike from Sully Creek south to the overlook above the Little Missouri is the most popular day hike along the Maah Daah Hey Trail.

ACCESS: To reach Sully Creek State Park from Medora, turn south from Pacific Avenue onto East River Road South. After 0.5 mile, the road turns to gravel. At 1.9 miles, turn right onto 36th Street at a sign for the park. There is parking at 2.4 miles at the beginning of the campground loop. For the Bully Pulpit trailhead (N46 52.477, W103 31.427) from Medora, turn south from Pacific Avenue onto East River Road South (DPG Road 3). Drive 3.1 miles south and turn right on Bible Camp Road, which may also be signed for the Bully Pulpit Golf Course. The Bully Pulpit trailhead is another 0.2 mile on the right at the entry to an oil well road. The Bible Camp Road intersection marks the end of the paved portion of DPG 3. For the Plumely Draw trailhead (N46 49.011, W103 30.334) from Medora, turn south from Pacific Avenue onto East River Road South (DPG Road 3). Pass Bible Camp Road and then cross the Maah Daah Hey Trail at 5.3 miles before reaching the Plumely Draw trailhead at 8.7 miles on the right. The Bully Pulpit and Plumely Draw trailheads have gravel parking, signboards, register boxes, and benches only. The Sully Creek Campground offers complete facilities for horses and other campers, including 41 campsites, vault toilets, pay showers, potable water, and a gravel parking area. This campground was electrified in the fall of 2019.

DISTANCE: This segment is 13.9 miles one-way.

ALLOWED USES: This trail is open to all non-motorized users, including hikers, mountain bikers, and horseback riders.

MAPS: Little Missouri National Grassland Maah Daah Hey National Recreation Trail 2018, Maah Daah Hey Trail Association Trail Guide (mdhta.com/trail-guide), Trails Illustrated Theodore Roosevelt National Park (#259), and USGS Chimney Butte, Tracy Mountain, and Medora, ND 7.5-minute quadrangles, and Map D.

The Plumely to Sully section of the Maah Daah Hey Trail is destined to become a favorite of mountain bikers and hikers because of its easy access to Medora and satisfying mix of badlands and grassland riding. Traveling this section south to north leaves riders with a long, exciting downhill finish and saves the easier and less technical riding for the end.

The trail begins immediately across the East River Road with a gentle climb eastward across the grassland. This section is marked with same wooden posts branded with the turtle symbol as the older Maah Daah Hey Trail. Some sections of the trail have gravel to protect the surface, but on others the trail tread is less obvious.

From the Plumely Draw trailhead (mile 33.3), ride east across the grassland. At mile 34.0, come to an old "road closed" sign and follow along an old two-track road up a small draw into some rugged badlands. At the head of the draw, circle around a small post-capped butte (N46 48.812, W103 28.693) at 35 miles and start to climb. Much of the slope along this climb slumped after the heavy rains of the spring of 2011, but has since been repaired.

Reach a grassland plateau and cross a self-closing gate. Enjoy some nice views north into Medora before starting a fun, twisty descent down some tight switchbacks. Reach another gate (N46 49.368, W103 27.614) on a lower-level grassland near MP 37. Exit this grassland on a long, swoopy descent, then cross under a powerline and over a two-track road. Shortly after a self-closing gate, reach the trail bridge over Davis Creek (N46 50.076, W103 27.025) at 38.5 miles.

From Davis Creek, make a hard right turn as the trail climbs north across a grassland littered with mammoth blocks of yellow sandstone. Once on the upper grassland, several oil wells are visible just east of the trail. Reach another gate just beyond MP 40 (N46 50.794, W103 27.494) then follow the fence line through a fun, twisty descent. It is obvious here how much effort the builders of the MDH put in to carve the trail into the steep badlands slopes.

At 41.6 miles, reach a gate on a narrow badlands ridge crest (N46 51.432, W103 28.658) and begin the well-earned descent down to the East River Road at 42.7 miles (N46 51.663, W103 29.759). Please use one of the designated trailheads for the Maah Daah Hey rather than parking at this trail crossing, as limited visibility makes parking here unsafe.

There's a short climb after crossing the road, but the trail then descends gradually down the rocky spine of a narrow ridge. At the next gate you can observe another area that slumped during the wet spring of 2011. Go straight across DPG Road 742-2 (N46 52.190, W103 30.839) near MP 44. Continue this exhilarating descent to reach Bible Camp Road (N46 52.499, W103 31.289) at 44.8 miles. To reach the trailhead, cross the road and ride west for 0.2 mile to the Bully Pulpit trailhead (N46 52.477, W103 31.427) which has a gravel parking area, signboard, and bench.

The connector between Bully Pulpit and Sully Creek was the last part of the Maah Daah Hey Trail to be constructed and this is now one of the trail's most scenic sections. Beyond Bible Camp Road, pass through a gate and along the shoulder of Bible Camp Road, then along the shoulder of DPG 3. Pull away from the road near the next gate and then begin an ascent past two swing gates before joining a plateau top two-track road that enters from the right. At MP 46 (N46 52.973, W103 32.073), there is a well-sited bench with sweeping views of both the Little Missouri River and the Bully Pulpit Golf Course. The trail next makes several broad switchbacks, including one exhilarating leg perched on the top of a sheer bluff above the river with tremendous views. Then descend through a cool, forested canyon past a stock tank on the right before reaching the Sully Creek trailhead at 47.2 miles (N46 53.402, W103 32.256). Just before entering the park via a swing gate, pass a large signboard listing the life members of the Maah Daah Hey Trail Association that was unveiled at the Trail's 20th Anniversary celebration in 2019.

Sully Creek State Park has perhaps the most elaborate facilities along the Maah Daah Hey Trail, a fitting reward for completing the southern portion of the MDH. There is ample camping for parties with or without horses, vault toilets, drinking water, and even a pay shower house. Sully Creek is also a convenient put-in or take-out area for river trips on the Little Missouri. There is a large signboard and map of the Maah Daah

Hey at the trailhead. At this kiosk just inside the Park is the original Mile Post 0, a stainless steel monument post showing the partners and legal location for the original MDH start point prior to the construction of the southern portion of the Maah Daah Hey Trail.

ABOVE Switchbacks and Scenic river views on the Maah Daah Hey Trail near Medora.

SULLY CREEK CAMPGROUND TO WANNAGAN CAMPGROUND, SULLY CREEK STATE PARK, MEDORA RANGER DISTRICT, AND THEODORE ROOSEVELT NATIONAL PARK, SOUTH UNIT

Exciting terrain, a variety of scenery, many fossils, and prolific wildlife make this a popular trip. The trail through the South Unit of Theodore Roosevelt National Park is closed to mountain bikes.

GENERAL LOCATION: Three miles south of Medora, North Dakota.

HIGHLIGHT: A scenic trail through one of America's best wildlife viewing parks.

ACCESS: To reach Sully Creek State Park from Medora, turn south from Pacific Avenue onto the paved East River Road South. At 1.8 miles, turn right onto 36th Street at a sign for the park. There is parking at 2.3 miles at the beginning of the campground loop (N46 53.402, W103 32.256). Parking is no longer permitted on the north side of the I-94 Exit 24 interchange. Hikers wishing to start at this point can park at Chimney Park in Medora and walk the 1.4 mile Medora Bike Path. Wannagan Campground can be reached from I-94 off Exit 23, three miles west of Medora. From Exit 23, turn north on gravel County Road 730. At 5.2 miles, a Forest Service road to the TRNP Petrified Forest trailhead splits right. At 7.9 miles, cross the Buffalo Gap Trail. At 9.7 miles, turn right onto DPG Road 726, which may not be signed. At 15.8 miles, keep right at the intersection with DPG Road 729. At 16.6 miles, just past the Wannagan trailhead on the right, turn left onto gravel DPG Road 726-15 which leads to the camp at 16.9 miles. Another option is a more direct route to Wannagan Camp from Sentinel Butte Exit 10 off I-94, heading east for three miles and then following DPG Road 726 for 14 miles.

ALLOWED USES: The trail in the national grassland is open to all non-motorized users, including hikers, mountain bikers, and

LEFT The Maah Daah Hey Trail along the Little Missouri River in TRNP.
ABOVE Approaching the Little Missouri River.

horseback riders. The trail through the South Unit of Theodore Roosevelt National Park is closed to mountain bikes, but bikers can use the Buffalo Gap Trail as a bypass.

DISTANCE: 17.6 miles one way.

MAPS: Little Missouri National Grassland Maah Daah Hey National Recreation Trail 2018, Maah Daah Hey Trail Association Trail Guide (mdhta.com/trail-guide) and Trails Illustrated Theodore Roosevelt National Park (#259). USGS Medora and Wannagan Creek East, ND 7.5-minute quadrangles, and Map D.

The southern section of the Maah Daah Hey Trail is perhaps its most diverse. Sully Creek State Park, Theodore Roosevelt National Park, and the Dakota Prairie Grasslands have combined to build a trail that highlights the best that the North Dakota badlands can offer. On this section you'll visit the trail's three main ecosystems: the lush river bottoms along the Little Missouri, stark badlands, and the surprisingly productive grasslands that surround them. The trip through the South Unit of Theodore Roosevelt National Park is one of the country's best wildlife walks. You'll likely see prairie dogs, bison, and pronghorn here, and possibly coyotes, deer, or elk as well.

The trail through the South Unit of Theodore Roosevelt National Park is closed to mountain bikes. Most of the South Unit, west of the Little Missouri River, is a designated wilderness area where mechanized travel is not permitted. To remedy this situation, the DPG built the Buffalo Gap Trail as a bypass route around the wilderness.

This section of the Maah Daah Hey Trail begins in Sully Creek State Park at the signboard 47.2 miles (N46 53.402, W103 32.256) and parking area near the campground entrance. Follow the wooden posts that mark the trail between the campground road and the Little Missouri River to a ford that is located across from the Little Muddy Breaks campground sites at 47.6 miles. During most years, crossing the sandy bottom here is relatively safe and easy by late spring. In other years, high water made the crossing dangerous until well into summer. Be sure to ask about water levels at the South Unit Visitor Center of TRNP, or get the data from the USGS water gauge data at Medora before committing to a river ford. The website is   https://waterdata.usgs.gov/nd/nwis/uv/?site_no=06336000&PARAmeter_cd=63158,00065,00060 for the Little Missouri River at Medora.

After one-quarter mile of sandy trail on private land on the west bank of the river, the trail crosses a two-track dirt road at a sign for a guest ranch near MP 48. Next, head west to a fence line where the trail begins a gradual climb up a small draw, then enters some well-developed badlands. Continue to climb up a scenic ridgeline until reaching the signed junction (N 46 54.319, W103 34.235) with the south end of the Buffalo Gap Trail at 49.3 miles at the crest of a divide. Here the Buffalo Gap Trail turns west to rejoin the MDH in 19.0 miles at MP 61.2 after bypassing the South Unit of Theodore Roosevelt National Park. In 2003, the DPG relocated part of the trail between the Buffalo Gap Trail junction and I-94 to both lessen grades on the Maah Daah Hey Trail and to avoid bighorn sheep habitat. An earlier relocation also changed the original trail route between Sully Creek and the Buffalo Gap junction. Both original routes are still shown on USGS base topographic maps.

From the Buffalo Gap Trail junction, the Maah Daah Hey Trail switchbacks north down past a stock pond into a gentle valley crossed by a two-track road. Across the valley are some sandstone boulders that provide welcome shade. The trail next climbs to a prairie ridgetop and passes through a gate just past MP 51. From the ridgeline, enjoy a long swooping descent into the valley of Andrews Creek with views of I-94 and Theodore Roosevelt National Park beyond. At 52.1 miles, reach the first of three closely-spaced gravel crossings of signed Andrews Creek. These crossings are usually easy, but may be muddy or difficult in high water. If needed, two crossings can be bypassed by bush whacking along the north bank of the creek.

Next cross a self-closing gate and then go under the railroad bridge. Reach the west end of Pacific Avenue at Exit 24 from I-94 at 52.5 miles (N46 55.807, W103 32.945) at a junction with the west end of the Medora

ABOVE Be sure to sign in at any trail registers you encounter in TRNP.

bike path, which leads 1.4 miles east to the Chimney Park in Medora. Trail users are no longer allowed to park at this interchange and the NPS warns hikers that vehicles left there will be ticketed. Instead, cross the road and look for a cluster of signs, including those for I-94, one indicating the end of the bike lane, and an arrow pointing right. The Maah Daah Hey Trail next follows a potentially muddy path between the interstate and the Little Missouri River, then passes underneath the bridges for both lanes of the interstate.

Debris piled around an interpretive sign for the MDH located directly under the eastbound lanes of I-94 is also a useful gauge of how high the river has crested during the prior spring runoff. Circle around the outside of the interchange to cross through a gate in a high bison fence at 52.8 miles (N46 55.992, W103 33.230) and turn north along the river. Once in the park, remember to give any wildlife a wide berth. It is likely that you will see bison grazing along the flat river bottom. A high fence line to the right shows the effects of bank erosion from the Little Missouri River as some sections of the fence have been undercut and tumbled to the river level, and other sections appear ready to soon join them. Cross through another fence opening at 53.2 miles (N46 56.252, W103 32.983).

ABOVE Trail junctions in Theodore Roosevelt NP are well-marked.

Beyond this fence, the MDH cuts across the wide sagebrush-studded bottom land of the Little Missouri River. By 53.6 miles the trail reaches the bluff line on the west side of the bottom land and will follow this bluff line north. Once across the bottom land, the trail follows a river terrace slightly higher in elevation and out of the tallest and densest growths of sagebrush, two factors that will help the trail surface stay drier. Some prairie wildflowers may be found here, including yarrow, salisfy, penstemon, and flax. At 54.6 miles (N46 57.116, W103 32.155), across the river from Cottonwood Campground and near the point where the bottomland has almost pinched out, reach a trail register box. This register box is a reminder of the park's earlier trail system, which included trail access to this point from the campground via a ford of the Little Missouri River.

At 55.2 miles (N46 57.487, W103 31.480), the trail makes a sharp left turn to leave the river bottom and climb up and over a small divide into the valley of Knutson Creek. The grassy valley of Knutson Creek is dotted with small groves of trees and offers appealing camping sites for those willing to treat water from Knutson Creek or the Little Missouri. At 55.6 miles (N46 57.781, W103 31.766), reach the signed junction with the Ekblom Trail, which enters on the right. The Ekblom Trail leads east 1.4 miles to Peaceful Valley trailhead via a ford of the Little Missouri River, and is described in more detail as part of the Lone Tree Loop Trail.

Walk west up the valley of Knutson Creek past more appealing campsites to a signed junction (N46 57.925, W103 32.113) with the Lone Tree Loop Trail, which is just past MP 56 and a bridged crossing of Knutson Creek. The Maah Daah Hey Trail bears right here to follow the east side of the loop on a 400-foot climb to Petrified Forest Plateau. The trail now is marked by posts bearing both the Maah Daah Hey and LT (for Lone Tree) brands. The trail enters a small prairie dog town as it follows a small branch of Knutson Creek north. You'll cross a small saddle and enjoy some welcome shade as the trail passes below the north side of a ridgeline as it approaches MP 57. The final climb to Petrified Forest Plateau goes through a rock layer containing fossilized tree stumps. At the top (N46 58.776, W103 32.162) at 57.2 miles, reach the intersection with the Big Plateau Trail which leads right 2.3 miles to the Peaceful Valley trailhead via a ford of the Little Missouri River.

Continue north on the combined trails, and at 57.4 miles reach the "V" junction with the South Petrified Forest Trail (N46 58.931, W103 32.265). Here the South Petrified Forest Trail branches slightly left, while the Maah Daah Hey Trail continues straight ahead on a glorious traverse of the grasslands atop the remarkably flat Petrified Forest Plateau. From this junction to the North Petrified Forest Trail, the Maah

Daah Hey Trail follows the Petrified Forest Loop as described in the TRNP chapter, but travels in the reverse direction.

Bear right from the "V" junction to reach the signed junction with the Mike Auney Trail (N46 59.205, W103 32.476) which enters from the right at 57.8 miles and leads to the Roundup Horse Camp in 2.8 miles via a ford of the Little Missouri River. Look for a small prairie dog town on the left between MPs 58 and 59 and keep an eye out for the bison, elk, and antelope that frequent this part of the plateau. The plateau here also features prolific wildflowers including pussy toes, penstemon, and vetch. The walk ahead is easy and scenic with views of the Little Missouri.

Follow the edge of the plateau until the ridge turns to the west and reach the junction with the Petrified Forest North Trail at 60.7 miles (N47 01.314, W103 33.538). To the left, the trail reaches the Petrified Forest trailhead in 3.3 miles via the Petrified Forest. The Maah Daah Hey Trail stays right and descends off the plateau to exit the park through a gate in a tall bison fence, then drops on switchbacks to reach the signed junction with the north end of the Buffalo Gap Trail at 61.2 miles at the south end of a large stock dam.

From this junction, the Buffalo Gap Trail leads left 19 miles south to rejoin the Maah Daah Hey Trail at 49.3 miles. The Buffalo Gap Trail offers a detour around the designated Wilderness Area in the South Unit of Theodore Roosevelt National Park, as well as access via the Buffalo Gap Connector Trail to the Buffalo Gap Campground and two others short trails starting from the campground.

The Maah Daah Hey Trail stays right and continues below the stock pond dam across state land through another mile of badlands. Then the trail follows a side draw toward Wannagan Creek. Reach a signed low-water crossing of Wannagan Creek and intersect the Wannagan Spur Trail before crossing gravel DPG Road 726 (N47 03.164, W103 35.120) at 64.5 miles. The Wannagan Spur Trail was completed in 2019 and leads 0.2 mile west on the south side of DPG 726 to the Wannagan trailhead, which was rehabilitated in 2019. Climb to a narrow ridge top to reach the signed junction with the Wannagan Trail at 64.8 miles (N47 03.164, W103 35.082). Follow the Wannagan Trail for 0.2 mile to the west to reach the campground (N47 03.335, W103 35.250).

Wannagan Campground has 10 sites, including large sites for horse parties, a hand pump for drinking water, and a gravel trailhead day-use lot. Camping is first come, first served. Wannagan is also a popular drop off point for riders using the Buffalo Gap and Maah Daah Hey Trails to ride into Medora. Commercial shuttles to Wannagan are also offered through Dakota Cyclery.

WANNAGAN CAMPGROUND TO ELKHORN CAMPGROUND, MEDORA RANGER DISTRICT

A challenging trail for hikers and mountain bikers through rolling grasslands and spectacular badlands.

GENERAL LOCATION: Fourteen miles northwest of Medora, North Dakota.

HIGHLIGHT: Scenic badlands are located at Ellison Creek and south of Crooked Creek.

ACCESS: Good maps are essential for reaching both trailheads. Wannagan Campground (N47 03.335, W103 35.250) can be reached from I-94 off Exit 23 three miles west of Medora. From Exit 23, turn north on gravel DPG Road 730. At 5.2 miles, keep left where a road to the TRNP Petrified Forest Westgate trailhead splits right. At 7.9 miles, cross the Buffalo Gap Trail. At 9.7 miles, turn right onto DPG Road 726, which may not be signed. At 15.8 miles, keep right at the intersection with DPG Road 729. At 16.6 miles, just past the Wannagan trailhead on the right, turn left onto gravel DPG Road 726-15, which leads to the camp at 16.9 miles.

Another option is a more direct route to Wannagan Camp. From Sentinel Butte, Exit 10 off I-94 heading east for three miles and then follow DPG Road 726 for 14 miles. Elkhorn Campground (N47 13.732, W103 39.950) can be reached by driving the first 15.8 miles of the route toward Wannagan Campground, then turning north on DPG Road 729 from Road 726. Stay left on Road 729 at the Road 728 junction, and then intersect gravel DPG Road 725 at 20.3 miles. Turn left and head west to reach the Bell Lake Road (DPG 708) at 23.8

ABOVE White Penstemon is also known as White Beardtongue.

miles. Follow the Bell Lake Road north to intersect DPG 2 at 35.5 miles. The Elkhorn Campground will be one mile down DPG 2, and the Theodore Roosevelt National Park Elkhorn Ranch will be two miles farther. Elkhorn Campground has eight campsites, some with good shade, vault toilets, and hand pumped potable water in season.

TRNP recommends a 27-mile long route to Elkhorn from I-94 at Exit 10. Turn left from the exit and follow County Road 11 north for 8.8 miles. Then, continue north on what will become Westerheim Road where 25th Street SW turns left. Ignore Elk Creek Road where it intersects from the left and reach the junction with Bell Lake Road (DPG 708) at 13.3 miles. Turn left and follow the Bell Lake Road north to the junction with DPG 2 at 24.8 miles. The Elkhorn Campground will be one mile down DPG 2 and the Theodore Roosevelt National Park Elkhorn Ranch will be two miles farther.

DISTANCE: 20.8 miles one way.

ALLOWED USES: This trail is open to all non-motorized users, including hikers, mountain bikers, and horseback riders.

MAPS: Little Missouri National Grassland Maah Daah Hey National Recreation Trail 2018, Maah Daah Hey Trail Association Trail Guide (mdhta.com/trail-guide) and Trails Illustrated Theodore Roosevelt National Park (#259). USGS Wannagan Creek East, Wannagan Creek West, and Roosevelt Creek West, ND, 7.5-minute quadrangles; and Map D.

Like much of the Maah Daah Hey Trail, the Wannagan to Elkhorn traverse challenges hikers with a long section in a remote area without reliable water. At the same time, it lures mountain bikers and horseback riders with the promise of uncrowded singletrack and with two scenic badlands areas sandwiched around a remote center of rolling grassland. Few hikers will be able to make this crossing in a single day, but except for the attractive sites at Crooked Creek and the unappealing sites near Roosevelt Creek, camping and water options are few. However, caching water at the Roosevelt Waterbox where the trail crosses County Road 722 will allow campers the luxury of choosing any site they please.

Early season visitors will find more tracks from pronghorns than humans. As with all sections of the Maah Daah Hey Trail, make sure that the water pumps are on at the camps before you head out, and keep an eye on the weather. Rain or damp conditions quickly turn the trail muddy. At its worst, even a short stretch of gumbo can be slick and sticky enough to stop bikers, horses, or hikers in their tracks. The weather here is more of a challenge than the terrain. Summer storms come up quickly, so any trail users should watch the weather for lightning. Since the only settings on North Dakota's thermostat are freeze and fry, there's little chance you'll be traveling in ideal conditions.

From the junction of the Maah Daah Hey Trail and the 0.2-mile side trail to Wannagan Camp at 64.8 miles, the trail heads north with a steep, spectacular climb up switchbacks to the ridge that dominates the view east from the camp. The next two miles feature an exquisite ridge-top traverse high above the Wannagan Creek badlands where partly submerged stumps of petrified wood litter the trail. The trail next turns north and drops into a pleasant, protected draw before crossing gravel DPG Road 728 (Cow Camp Road) (N47 04.764, W103 36.675) at 67.8 miles. The trail uses a few switchbacks to drop into another small draw south of MP 69 where camping is possible.

North of this draw, the Maah Daah Hey Trail traverses west along the crest of a thin ridge with exceptional badlands vistas. North of this ridge, however, the trail begins to move further west of the Little Missouri River so that badlands formations are not as well developed. However, the trail soon crosses Crooked Creek (N47 06.428, W103 36.973) at 71.4 miles and reaches flat and scenic campsites. Here you are likely to see more wild turkey than cattle, and a bit of exploration should reveal a few pieces of petrified wood.

The Maah Daah Hey Trail next climbs to cross gravel DPG Road 725 (Roosevelt Creek/Short Road) (N47 06.949, W103 37.669) at 72.4 miles and begins a long traverse of open grassland. While gradually descending toward Roosevelt Creek, the trail passes both a remarkably huge stock dam and an active oil well to the east of the trail. The north bank of Roosevelt Creek offers small campsites in the trees, but will probably have cattle in summer. The cattle likely are attracted by the flowing well and stock tank found at the signed creek crossing (N47 08.261, W103 38.911) just short of MP 75. The wide crossing can be muddy. From Roosevelt Creek, the trail climbs to a ridge overlooking a new road leading to an oil well before dropping to cross gravel DPG Road 722 at 76.8 miles. The Roosevelt Waterbox is located about 200 feet north of the road (N47 09.381, W103 38.997).

Hike alongside DPG Road 722 to the west before climbing north to a ridge top and two-track road that leads to a stock tank. Continue on the ridge top to cross a gravel road to an oil well. Switchback off the ridge to reach the bottom of a small draw. Climb from the draw to reach another stock tank near the intersection with some faint ranch roads. After a short time on the divide, descend toward Dry Creek. The south fork of Dry Creek is a long, narrow gash in the earth, an erosional feature more typical of South Dakota's Badlands National Park than of the Little Missouri badlands. Here the process of stream erosion has acted swiftly and violently to carve a deep, straight channel through soft bedrock. Cross the signed Dry Creek at 81.2 miles (N47 11.672, W103 39.643). The creek bottom is too dry and narrow for camping.

After Dry Creek, the Maah Daah Hey Trail moves closer to the Little Missouri River and again passes through well-developed badlands terrain. There is a faint ranch road on the next divide north and a stock dam and grassy two-track road in the following draw. Cross over one gentler divide to reach the signed crossing of Ellison Creek (N47 12.903, W103 39.963) at 83.3 miles near a pond. Hike east down the creek, then turn left up a side draw at a large stock pond. Cross a Forest Service oilfield road at 84.7 miles. Enjoy views of the surrounding badlands before descending toward the Elkhorn Campground. At 85.6 miles, you can turn left to enter the campground through a self-closing gate where the MDH turns sharply right at the signed junction with the Elkhorn Trail (N47 13.732, W103 39.950). The Elkhorn Trail turns left here to reach Elkhorn Camp, with a water well, picnic tables, and some shade, alongside DPG 2 in 0.3 mile. The Maah Daah Hey Trail turns east and runs along the south side of DPG 3 to reach the Elkhorn trailhead at 86 miles.

ABOVE Magpie Trailhead.
LEFT Pronghorn are common in the North Dakota Badlands.

ELKHORN CAMPGROUND TO MAGPIE CAMPGROUND, MEDORA RANGER DISTRICT

A pleasant walk or ride through the Buckhorn and Devils Pass oilfields, which includes a ford of the Little Missouri River.

GENERAL LOCATION: About 36 miles northwest of Medora, North Dakota.

HIGHLIGHT: Theodore Roosevelt's Elkhorn Ranch Site, and the spectacular crossing of Devils Pass.

ACCESS: Elkhorn Campground (N47 13.732, W103 39.950) can be reached by driving the first 15.8 miles of the route toward Wannagan Campground, then turning north on DPG Road 729 from Road 726, until it intersects gravel DPG Road 728 at 17.2 miles. Stay left on Road 729 at the DPG Road 728 junction and then intersect gravel DPG Road 725 at 20.3 miles. Turn left and head west to reach the Bell Lake Road (DPG 708) at 23.8 miles. Follow the Bell Lake Road north to intersect DPG 2 at 35.5 miles. The Elkhorn Campground will be one mile down DPG 2 and the Theodore Roosevelt National Park Elkhorn Ranch will be two miles farther.

The Elkhorn Campground has eight campsites, some with good shade, vault toilets, and potable water in season. TRNP recommends a 27-mile long route to Elkhorn from I-94 at Exit 10. Turn left from the exit and follow County Road 11 north for 8.8 miles. Then continue north on what will become Westerheim Road where 25th Street SW turns left. Ignore Elk Creek Road where it intersects from the left and reach the junction with Bell Lake Road (DPG 708) at 13.3 miles. Turn left and follow the Bell Lake

Road north to the junction with DPG 2 at 24.8 miles. The Elkhorn Campground will be one mile down DPG 2, and the Theodore Roosevelt National Park Elkhorn Ranch will be two miles farther.

For the nearest road access to the Little Missouri River crossing, continue north on DPG Road 708. One mile north of the turn off for Elkhorn Campground, DPG 2 will split left and north while DPG 708 goes right. Follow DPG 708 for another 4.5 miles to where it crosses the MDH near MP 93 for the closest river access on the trail. For four-wheel drive vehicle access, follow DPG 708 for one mile then right on DPG 703 for one mile then right to the Little Missouri River crossing. Cross the river, then follow DPG 712 north for 3/4 mile then east for about 10 miles to Magpie Campground (N47 18.478, W103 28.360).

Magpie Campground can be found by driving west 15.5 miles on DPG Road 712 (Magpie Road) from US 85 about 1.5 miles north of the town site of Fairfield. On well-graded DPG 712, pass DPG 795 on the left at 2.9 miles, Blair Road (DPG 717) on the left at 6.8 miles, Goat Pass Road (DPG 711) on the left at 11.5 miles, oilfield roads on the left (13.4 miles) and right (13.6 miles), DPG 712-6 is on the left at 14.7 miles, and the Magpie trailhead is on the right at 14.9 miles before reaching the 0.5-mile long campground road on the right at 15.5 miles. Magpie Campground has eight sites, vault toilets and a potable water pump in season. Magpie trailhead has a gravel parking area, signboard, and register box.

DISTANCE: 19.7 miles one way.

ALLOWED USES: This trail is open to all non-motorized users, including hikers, mountain bikers, and horseback riders.

MAPS: Little Missouri National Grassland Maah Daah Hey National Recreation Trail 2018, Maah Daah Hey Trail Association Trail Guide (mdhta.com/trail-guide) and Trails Illustrated Theodore Roosevelt National Park (#259). USGS Roosevelt Creek West, Eagle Draw, Hanks Gully, and Squaretop Butte, ND 7.5-minute quadrangles; and Map D.

The section of the Maah Daah Hey Trail around the Little Missouri River is one of the most diverse. Much of the trail is intertwined with a maze of gravel roads that service the area's oil wells, but the trail makes up for this intrusion with some nice campsites and perhaps its most scenic feature: the rough and narrow crossing of Devils Pass. Here also is perhaps the trail's biggest potential obstacle, the crossing of the Little Missouri River. In most years, the crossing is nothing worse than a place to get your feet wet. However, during the spring runoff the river levels are uncertain. It is best to check with the staff at Theodore Roosevelt National Park to make sure the water is not too high, or get the data from the USGS water gauge data at Medora before committing to a river ford. The website is   https://waterdata.usgs.gov/nd/nwis/uv/?site_no=06336000&PARAmeter_cd=63158,00065,00060. A waterbox on Magpie Road (DPG 712) near MP 98 should be enough to help hikers complete this long section (N47 17.813, W103 34.452).

During his ranching days, Theodore Roosevelt kept his main ranch at Elkhorn near the start of this section. The site is preserved as part of Theodore Roosevelt National Park, but has not been developed. This ranch site is discussed in more detail in the chapter on Theodore Roosevelt National Park.

The section begins at the junction of the Maah Daah Hey and Elkhorn Trails. Elkhorn Camp (N47 13.732, W103 39.950) is 0.1 mile to the west along the Elkhorn Trail at 85.6 miles. From the junction, the Maah Daah Hey turns east and crosses gravel DPG Road 2 at the Elkhorn trailhead. Just short of MP 86, the trail crosses a two-track dirt road, then closely follows the north side of DPG 2. At 86.4 miles, there is a flowing well just south of the trail. At 87.6 miles, the trail reaches the edge of the bottomland along the Little Missouri River next to the parking area for the Elkhorn Ranch Unit of Theodore Roosevelt National Park (N47 14.072, W103 37.757). A flowing well is located just south and east of the trail.

The Elkhorn Ranch Unit of TRNP is undeveloped, but visitors are welcome to wander the area. A gate in the National Park Service fence at the parking area leads to a mowed path. By taking a left at a T-junction, this path will lead to the ranch and blacksmith sites near the river. Roosevelt described his home ranch as a "long, low house of hewn logs" with a line of cottonwoods in front for shade. He described the ranch as always cool and pleasant during the fierce heat of summer, and in winter choked with blazing fires to thwart the season's iron desolation. Roosevelt was an active rancher, joining his men in the chores of riding, roping, and roundup. He was active in stockowners groups, giving early warnings against the perils of overgrazing, and forecasted the devastation that the winter of 1886–1887 would wreak on the cattle herds.

From Elkhorn Ranch Parking Area, the Maah Daah Hey Trail turns north and climbs above the river. There is a stock tank in a small draw and another spring-fed tank just before the trail makes its first crossing of DPG Road 708 at 89.1 miles (N47 14.911, W103 38.697). The trail follows the east side of DPG 708 for a quarter mile before turning north to drop into pretty Morgan Draw. The trail follows down the draw to cross a gravel road that leads to an oil well at a feeding station for cattle. Continue past a flowing well and stock tank, and then down the draw before beginning the 200-foot climb up to a flat, windswept tableland at MP 92.

Head northeast across the tableland and pass an old corral before dropping to the second, more northern crossing on DPG Road 708 at 93.1 miles (N47 16.594, W103 37.232). This is the closest road access to the trail's crossing of the Little Missouri River. Descend on switchbacks to the river bottomland where shaded camping is possible. Turn north and reach the ford of the Little Missouri at 94.1 miles (N47 16.874, W103 36.967). On the west bank bluffs, look for a prominent black lignite layer in the exposed bedrock and for pieces of lignite in the river gravels.

After making the ford, cross through a self-closing gate onto state land where you are required to stay on the trail for the next 0.5 mile. Reach a signed crossing of Whitetail Creek. In high water, this crossing could be difficult and wet. Hike along the north bank of the creek through a pretty grove of cottonwood trees at MP 95. After you

ABOVE Hikers and mountain bike riders share the Maah Daah Hey Trail.

cross onto the DPG property, look for potential campsites in the trees that offer shade and fresh water, a combination that will be difficult to match in the next few miles. Turn left and away from the creek and cross through a self-closing gate, then reach DPG 719A (N47 17.056, W103 35.407). Cross the road at 95.6 miles after an oil well service road branches north and begin to climb.

Near the top of the steep route full of switchbacks is the former site of the post that marked the midway point of the Maah Daah Hey Trail prior to the construction of the southern portion at 96.5 miles. The post listed the names of trail coordinator Curt Glasoe, crew chief Russ Walsh, and the crew and Partners (ND Parks and Recreation, National Park Service, and LMNG) that constructed the trail. Enjoy your last view of the river on this section and head north on a high plateau. Cross through another self-closing gate on a very narrow ridge line before reaching DPG Road 712 near an oil well at 97.4 miles (N47 17.870, W103 34.813).

North Dakota's oilfields are part of a geologic structure called the Williston Basin, a 300,000-square-mile feature centered in the western part of the state. Oil was first discovered here in 1951. Production and exploration have followed the same ups and downs common to the rest of the energy industry, with bursts of activity following advances in technology, new discoveries, and events such as the 1970s OPEC oil embargo. Over half the oil comes from rocks of the Mississippian Madison Group, very similar to the rocks that make up the Limestone Plateau in South Dakota's Black Hills. North Dakota's statewide production of 461 million barrels of crude oil in 2018 was the second highest in the United States following Texas, and ten times the production rate of 2006. Much of the production increase comes via new technologies, such as hydraulic fracturing (fracking), that enable increased production of oil and gas that were previously not economical to extract.

Hike east beside DPG Road 712 and reach the Magpie waterbox south of the DPG 712 and MDH trail at 97.8 miles (N47 17.813, W103 34.452) before winding south around a small butte and then crossing the road. The Magpie waterbox is five miles west of the Magpie Campground on DPG Road 712, and a total of 20.5 miles west of US 85 on DPG Road 712.

After the road turns north, veer away from it to the west to cross a small ridge in a section marked by patches of gumbo and the signs of an old burn. Recross DPG Road 712. A grove of juniper and aspen could make a nice campsite. The trail next traverses the edge of a plateau high above the rugged Whitetail Creek badlands. Reach a junction with a well-worn two-track road at a self-closing gate and a sign for Devils Pass at 100.6 miles. The pass (N47 17.698, W103 32.249) is a narrow sliver of upland that is the only connection between the badlands along Whitetail Creek to the south and those along Magpie Creek to the north. This was the original access route to the western badlands from the east for early settlers, and it was closed to vehicle use in the early 1980s. Leave the road to the left and make the crossing of Devils Pass while enjoying the views of the steep, rugged badlands on either side.

Soon, recross the old two-track road and then pass a dry stock dam. At 101.5 miles is a small dam with water (N47 17.487, W103 31.333) and a potential campsite down the trail. Climb from the pond up to DPG Road 711 (N47 17.274, W103 30.741) near the junction with a large oil well and DPG Road 711-6. Cross DPG Road 711 for the final time at 102.2 miles and descend a narrow, shaded draw. There is a spring-fed stock tank just south of the trail before crossing another self-closing gate. Crest a small divide to reach a stock pond. Next, cross gravel DPG Road 712-10 (N47 17.920, W103 29.821) and pass just south of a tiny butte. Pass a huge oil well on the right, and cross a self-closing gate before reaching DPG Road 712 and the Magpie trailhead at 105.2 miles (N47 18.229, W103 28.537), just north of a split in the road and a cattle guard. The trailhead has a gravel parking area, a signboard, and a register box. Enter the wide valley of Magpie Creek and continue east to reach the junction with the signed side trail to Magpie Campground at 105.3 miles (N47 18.260, W103 28.346). The Magpie Trail turns north to reach the campground in 0.4 mile (N47 18.478, W103 28.360). There are some spectacular rock formations in the drainage just north of the trail junction with the MDH trail. The Magpie Campground has 10 sites, a latrine, hand pump for drinking water, and horse tie ups. This campground has plenty of trees, providing mostly shaded campsites. Because of the appeal of shaded campsites and its location east of Devils Pass and west of the Ice Caves, this is the most used campground on the MDH. Both the Ice Caves and Devils Pass are within day-hike distance from Magpie Campground.

The Little Missouri badlands have a scenic beauty all their own. The landscape is a mix of shortgrass prairie and seemingly barren badlands. It is a terrain that combines sweeping vistas with often overlooked wildflowers, rock formations, and wildlife among the sculpted coulees and grassy tablelands. The grasslands are a chaotic patchwork of public and private land. Thus, it cannot support the diversity of wildlife seen in Theodore Roosevelt National Park, but mule deer, pronghorn, coyotes, and prairie dogs are common. Lucky visitors might spy rare elk, whitetail deer, or bighorn sheep.

RIGHT A small grove of trees provides shade north of Magpie Creek.

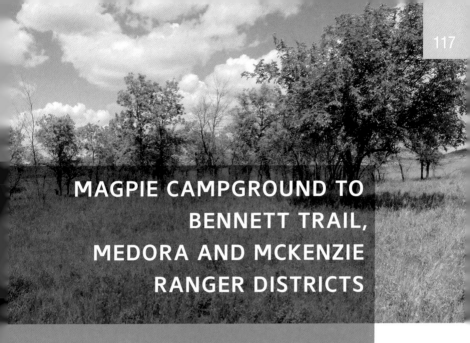

MAGPIE CAMPGROUND TO BENNETT TRAIL, MEDORA AND MCKENZIE RANGER DISTRICTS

A long, lonely mix of prairie and badlands open to hikers, mountain bikers, and horseback riders.

GENERAL LOCATION: Eight miles west of Grassy Butte, North Dakota.

HIGHLIGHT: A remote setting sprinkled with many petrified wood deposits.

ACCESS: Magpie Campground can be found by driving west 15.5 miles on DPG Road 712 (Magpie Road) from US 85 about 1.5 miles north of the town site of Fairfield. On well-graded DPG Road 712, pass DPG 795 on the left at 2.9 miles, Blair Road (DPG 717) on the left at 6.8 miles, Goat Pass Road (DPG 711) on the left at 11.5 miles, oilfield roads on the left (13.4 miles) and right (13.6 miles), DPG 712-6 on the left at 14.7 miles, and the Magpie trailhead on the right at 14.9 miles before reaching the 0.5-mile long campground road on the right at 15.5 miles. Magpie Campground has 10 sites, vault toilets and a potable water pump in season. Magpie trailhead has a gravel parking area, signboard, and register box.

To reach the Beicegel Creek waterbox, use McKenzie County Road 50 (DPG Road 7, also called the Beicegel Creek Road) that leaves US 85 15.5 miles south of the entrance to the North Unit of TRNP at the small community of Grassy Butte. Drive west on County Road 50 6.5 miles past the crossing of the MDH to DPG 809, then 0.3 mile south on DPG 809 to another crossing of the MDH where the box is on the right (west side of the road).

County Road 50 is paved for at least seven miles west to the crossing of the Maah Daah Hey Trail. If you reach a junction with DPG 809 heading south, then you've passed the trail crossing.

To reach Bennett Campground from US 85 7.5 miles north of Grassy Butte, turn west onto the gravel Bennett Creek Road (aka 6th Street NW), at a sign for the campground. At 4.0 miles, turn left onto signed DPG 824. At 4.5 miles, turn right onto DPG 824-4 at a sign for the campground. Reach the Bennett trailhead at 5.3 miles. There is gravel parking at the Bennett trailhead with a signboard and register box. The Bennett Campground (N47 29.444, W103 21.083) has 13 sites, a hand pump for drinking water, and is accessible from the MDH off a spur of the Bennett Trail.

DISTANCE: 22.1 miles one way.

ALLOWED USES: This trail is open to all non-motorized users, including hikers, mountain bikers, and horseback riders.

MAPS: Little Missouri National Grassland Maah Daah Hey National Recreation Trail 2018, Maah Daah Hey Trail Association Trail Guide (mdhta.com/trail-guide) and Trails Illustrated Theodore Roosevelt National Park (#259) USGS Squaretop Butte, Wolf Coulee, and Buckskin Butte, ND 7.5-minute quadrangles; and Map D.

This long stretch of the Maah Daah Hey Trail illustrates how isolated the North Dakota badlands can be. In 22 miles, the trail crosses only one lonely paved road that probably sees a few vehicles a day. But where people are rare, wildlife is more common. This is a good trail to take if you're after sightings of mule deer, pronghorn antelope, or migrating birds. As a bonus, there are two options for loop trips on this section. The Bennett and Cottonwood trails make a 15.1-mile loop all on singletrack at the north end of this section. A 20.7-mile loop that combines 10 miles of Maah Daah Hey Trail, 1.5 miles of the Ice Caves Trail, plus 10 miles of little-traveled gravel DPG Roads 808 and 809 would provide some easier riding than a purely singletrack route.

One of the joys of the Maah Daah Hey Trail is the diversity of terrain. The easiest walking is on the high, flat grasslands where the views stretch to the horizon and the wildlife watching is the best. The few creeks that drain this arid land offer shelter, food, and water for wildlife. But the most visually stunning areas are the badlands, where the forces of falling water have sculpted a wild and unique terrain. Between County Road 50 and Bennett Creek, the Maah Daah Hey Trail explores all three of these ecosystems. Should you have time to visit only part of the trail, this section will show you what the trail is about and will lure you back to explore its entire length.

From the junction with the Magpie Trail at 105.3 miles (N47 18.260, W103 28.346), the Maah Daah Hey Trail heads east to a normally easy crossing of signed Magpie Creek. On the north side of the creek, cross an old two-track road which connects an old corral on the left with an old ranch building on the right. Beyond the creek, crest a gentle hill and pass a small pond nestled in a shaded grove on the left. Cross through a self-closing gate and drop into a deep, dry wash lined with cottonwoods. The trail crosses another old two-track road before reaching a flowing well, stock tank, and weed-covered pond next to a corral. Keep right of a fence line until the trail crosses the fence at a self-closing gate. Then loop around the pond to a second gate.

After crossing a dry gulch, pass a small butte where fragments of petrified wood and lignite are eroding from a layer of bentonite. Pass a self-closing gate before reaching the confluence of two small washes where you may find water in shallow puddles. As the trail begins to climb, reach the junction with the Ice Caves Trail at 108.6 miles (N47 18.921, W103 25.018). The Ice Caves Trail leads 0.6 mile east to the caves and 1.5 miles to the Ice Caves trailhead, located off DPG Road 808. The 0.3-mile Aspen Trail forms a short loop with the Ice Caves Trail near the caves. The Ice Caves and Aspen trails are described in detail in the following chapter.

From the Ice Caves Trail junction, the Maah Daah Hey Trail keeps left and then passes to the west and then north of a butte with an elevation of 2,556 feet. Notice how the hard caprock on top of the butte protects it from erosion and allows it to remain standing high above the surrounding landscape. There is a small arch along the trail north of the butte. Next, pass a large oilfield development on the right.

After crossing a small gully, reach MP 110. In another 100 yards, cross a gate that marks the McKenzie-Billings county line, which is also the boundary between the Medora and McKenzie Ranger Districts in the Little Missouri National Grassland. Cross one more coulee, which may be home to skittish mule deer, and enjoy some flat, easy walking along the level ridgetop. Leave the ridge at a north-facing notch and descend toward a small pond opposite a bread loaf-shaped butte. Cross a dry tributary of Beicegel Creek at a self-closing gate near MP 113. You'll catch a glimpse of gravel DPG Road 809 to the west as you climb to a small divide capped with a concrete tank that likely is dry at 113.5 miles.

Cross little-traveled gravel DPG Road 809 at 114.9 miles (N47 22.648, W103 24.264). Just north of the road is a stock pond rimmed with cottonwoods that could provide an emergency supply of water.

But Beicegel Creek at 115.4 miles (N47 22.972, W103 28.24.221) is just beyond, and there is often a modest water flow in the springtime. The creek bottom is lined with lignite bands, and exposed stumps of fossilized trees are strewn about. On the north bank of the creek, a nearby grove of cottonwoods would also provide a nice campsite.

North of Beicegel Creek is a long hike across a gumbo-covered flat that could be hellishly sticky walking in wet weather. On the far end of the flat is a dry stock tank by the trail and a stock pond off to the right near MP 116. Look for more fragments of petrified wood on the climb away from the flat. Soon after, reach a high grassy tableland. Watch for the fleet, bounding forms of pronghorn here.

The pronghorn, commonly called antelope, is a uniquely American animal; the species has no close relatives. Both males and females have horns, but those of the female are shorter and are rarely pronged. If you can get close enough, you can also distinguish the males by black patches on the lower jaw and by a black mask extending back from the nose. Pronghorns are North America's speed kings. They've been clocked at 60 miles per hour and can sustain speeds of 30-40 mph. Pronghorn are one of the state's most popular game animals. North Dakota's Game and Fish Department estimates the population at around 12,000 animals.

Leave the tableland at the head of an aspen-filled draw. Down the draw is a pretty pond with relatively clean water and inviting camping just short of MP 118. Canadian geese also appreciate this site. After passing Hanson Overlook, reach the Beicegel Creek Road waterbox on the left just before crossing DPG Road 809 at 119.2 miles (N47 124.780, W103 22.686). The forest service completed a short trail to the overlook in the fall of 2019. The luxury of a short, mostly paved access road makes this the most convenient waterbox along the Maah Daah Hey Trail. Reach a self-closing gate and enter a section of state land where travelers need to stay on the trail for the next 1.5 miles. Cross paved McKenzie County Road 50 (DPG Road 7) (N47 25.170, W103 21.878) at 120.1 miles.

From County Road 50, hike north up and over a small ridge crest. Descend into a narrow draw where a piped spring supplying a stock tank may provide water. The grove of cottonwoods below the tank makes a fine resting spot. Continue north along the narrow valley until you leave the state land and begin a switched back climb. Crest the rim of a broad tableland. A small aspen grove on the west edge of the table hides a small, partly filled pond.

Reach the signed intersection with the Cottonwood Trail at 122.4 miles (N47 26.605, W103 21.487). This trail was built in 2005 and substantially repaired after damage from the extremely wet spring of

2011. The Cottonwood Trail leads north 7.0 miles to a junction with the Bennett Trail, just 0.3 mile west of Bennett Campground. The 15-mile loop hike with the Cottonwood, Maah Daah Hey, and Bennett Trails is described in detail in the next chapter.

Keep left at the junction to stay on the Maah Daah Hey Trail and pass one more stock tank while following the narrow extension of the tableland to the north on some fun, fast riding. To the east is Cottonwood Creek. Enjoy some good creek views before dropping off the north end of the tableland on some switchbacks. Pass another stock tank before crossing the usually dry west fork of Cottonwood Creek at MP 124 (N47 27.599, W103 22.118). The Maah Daah Hey Trail then follows the west bank of the creek and crosses several small coulees.

Cross through a self-closing gate at 124.5 miles, which may mark the upper limit of water in Cottonwood Creek. On the next small divide is a petrified wood locality, which also offers some broader vistas. Next, pass another small pond before turning up a side coulee at 125.5 miles to avoid crossing the very deep canyon of another west fork of Cottonwood Creek. As of 2020, the DPG plans a slight reroute of the trail near this crossing. The trail continues north along Cottonwood Creek. Then the terrain turns monotonously flat and is covered in dense sagebrush. At 126.7 miles, cross the dry bed of another Cottonwood Creek tributary.

Reach the signed junction with the Bennett Trail at 127.4 miles (N47 29.578, W103 23.687) just before leaving Cottonwood Creek to the west near the confluence with Bennett Creek and at another petrified wood locality. The Bennett Trail leads 3.1 miles east along the south side of Bennett Creek to Bennett Campground (N47 29.444, W103 21.083) and DPG Road 824. There is a good low water crossing at Bennett Creek. Bennett Trail is marked with a bighorn sheep head symbol on posts similar to those used for the Maah Daah Hey Trail. The Bennett Campground has a gravel parking area, 13 campsites, a latrine, a signboard, register box, and hand pump for water.

BENNETT TRAIL TO CCC CAMPGROUND, MCKENZIE RANGER DISTRICT & THEODORE ROOSEVELT NATIONAL PARK, NORTH UNIT

After climbing the spectacular China Wall, this section combines Collar Draw and Corral Creek with high grasslands along Long X Divide. *The two miles of this trail in the North Unit of Theodore Roosevelt National Park are closed to mountain bikes.*

GENERAL LOCATION: Four miles south of the North Unit of Theodore Roosevelt National Park.

HIGHLIGHT: The China Wall, views from Long X Divide, and the chance to see bison at Corral Creek.

ACCESS: From US 85, 7.5 miles north of Grassy Butte, turn west onto the gravel Bennett Creek Road (aka 6th Street NW) at a sign for the Bennett Campground. At 4.0 miles, turn left onto signed DPG 824. At 4.5 miles, turn right onto DPG 824-4 at a sign for the campground. Reach the Bennett trailhead at 5.3 miles. There is gravel parking at the Bennett trailhead with a signboard and register box. The Bennett Campground (N47 29.444, W103 21.083) has 13 sites, a hand pump for drinking water, and is accessible off the MDH on a spur of the Bennett Trail.

From US 85 just 0.8 mile south of the North Unit entrance and immediately south of the bridge over the Little Missouri River, turn west onto DPG 842 at signs for the CCC Campground. Stay right at a cattle guard at 0.9 mile and enter the campground at 1.1 miles. Pass the starts of loops C (left), A (right), and B (left) to reach the Maah Daah Hey trailhead (N47 35.182, W103 16.735) at 1.3 miles.

LEFT Yellow "Hymenoxys" sunflowers and white penstemon at Wind Canyon.
ABOVE Badlands scenery along Cottonwood Creek.

The trailhead has a gravel parking area, signboard, and register box. The campground has 38 camp sites, a picnic shelter, latrine, and a hand pump for drinking water. The CCC Trail (N47 35.113, W103 16.389) leaves from the end of loop C at a trail register by a signpost and self-closing gate to connect to the MDH in 0.3 mile at MP 144.

DISTANCE: 16.9 miles one way.

ALLOWED USES: The trail in the national grassland is open to all non-motorized users, including hikers, mountain bikers, and horseback riders. Mountain bikes are not allowed in Theodore Roosevelt National Park.

MAPS: Little Missouri National Grassland Maah Daah Hey National Recreation Trail 2018, Maah Daah Hey Trail Association Trail Guide (mdhta.com/trail-guide) and Trails Illustrated Theodore Roosevelt National Park (#259), USGS Wolf Coulee, Sperati Point, and Long X Divide, ND 7.5-minute quadrangles; and Map D.

The northern section of the Maah Daah Hey Trail is one of its more unusual. This section sees much use by horses taking advantage of the Dakota Prairie Grassland's CCC Campground and the Long X Trail. However, mountain bikers are presented with a logistical problem in this section: bikers are prohibited by wilderness regulations from riding on the trail in the North Unit of Theodore Roosevelt National Park. Instead of attempting to ride the entire Maah Daah Hey Trail, mountain bikers often will simply ride the MDH from Bennett Campground south to the Burning Coal Vein Campground via the Buffalo Gap Trail.

However, this also is one of the trail's most scenic sections. It starts with a ride alongside, then up and over the China Wall, a badlands formation that for many is the highlight of their trip. Hikers and horseback riders will enjoy their brief brush with designated wilderness in TRNP's North Unit.

Beyond the intersection with the Bennett Trail at 127.4 miles (N47 29.444, W103 21.083), reach a small stock tank and a nearly weed-filled pond as you turn west up a side coulee. The north side of this coulee is called the China Wall. This imposing climb begins beyond MP 128 where the DPG plans a slight reroute of the trail, and follows a steep badlands divide toward Bennett Creek. The wall is mix of cream and terra cotta towers and turrets. The soft rock here is so vulnerable to erosion that the wall may look different every time you visit. Be prepared: the descent is every bit as steep as the climb. Ride through sagebrush flats north of the Wall to a signed crossing of Bennett Creek. The land north of China Wall is part of an oil patch, and you'll see many signs of energy development here. Reach gravel DPG Road 823 at MP 130 (N47 30.337, W103 24.532) in between the intersections of DPG Road 823 and two oilfield roads. DPG Road 823 is not a viable route for bypassing the Wilderness Area in the North Unit of Theodore Roosevelt National Park as it is signed as a private road 2.5 miles to the east.

From DPG Road 823, the Maah Daah Hey Trail climbs alongside DPG 823. Beyond DPG 823, the trail makes a sharp turn to the west and switches back to climb to a long, narrow tableland where it parallels a two-track dirt road to the north. Drop off the west side of the tableland where the trail leaves the road and head north along Collar Draw.

Pass a small pond at 132.4 miles (N47 31.862, W103 24.466) with a flat area beyond it that provides some pretty camping spots. Beyond the pond, the Maah Daah Hey Trail follows the remains of a well-worn two-track road. Pass a stock tank before reaching perhaps the most remarkable fossil site along the entire trail. Here a five-foot-tall stump of petrified wood lies on its side. The stump is attached to a five-foot-diameter circular root system that makes the fossil resemble a huge, white mushroom turned to stone.

The fossil wood found in Theodore Roosevelt National Park and the surrounding Dakota Prairie Grasslands is most often found at the base of the Sentinel Butte Formation. Scientists believe that the trees were conifers, similar to modern sequoias. Some specimens are huge, with diameters approaching eight feet. Since the root systems of the trees are typically poorly preserved, the trees probably grew in a swampy environment, similar to cypress groves of today. Visitors are not allowed to collect fossil wood in the national park.

A six-foot-high bison fence marks the boundary of the North Unit of Theodore Roosevelt National Park at 133.6 miles (N47 32.692, W103 24.575). Since this part of the park has been designated a Wilderness Area, mountain bikes are not allowed here. Unfortunately, there is not a contiguous zone of public access around the North Unit, so there is yet no approved bypass route around the park. From the park fence, the Little Missouri River, a guaranteed source of water, is one mile of bushwhacking to the west. The park section of the trail is marked by the same large posts that mark other TRNP trails.

The trail along Corral Creek explores a flat valley bottom crowded with giant sagebrush. However, there are nice views to the north of the buttes capping the Achenbach Hills, and there is always a chance of sighting one of the bison that frequent the creek bottom.

The Maah Daah Hey Trail leaves the park at 135.4 miles (N47 32.675, W103 22.681) at a gate through the bison fence. Continue up the valley of Corral Creek until the valley begins to narrow. Make the crossing of the banks of Corral Creek then turn abruptly south and climb on switchbacks up a wooded slope toward Long X Divide. The trail from MP 135-137 was reconstructed in 2003 to lessen grades and ease the creek crossing. Keep climbing past MP 137 before reaching the level grasslands on Long X Divide near a stock tank. Near MP 138 the trail crosses a fence with a self-closing gate and heads due east along the section line.

You'll pass two more gates and a stock tank on the right before coming to the intersection with the west end of the 5.8-mile Long X Trail and DPG Road 825 at 138.8 miles (N47 32.724, W103 19.393). The Long X Trail turns left along the dirt road and is marked with posts branded with a large X. It provides an alternate route to the CCC Campground which is described in detail in the next chapter. From the fence corner, DPG 825 bears right, and there is a waterbox at the junction. The Maah Daah Hey Trail continues straight ahead to the east. MP 139 is within sight ahead, and a welcome patch of shade lies just beyond.

The trail soon parallels the two-track road and follows it to the northeast across the sunny tableland. After entering state lands, the trail moves west of the two-track road briefly, rejoins it, then passes a stock tank. Near MP 140, a stock tank and pond lie on opposite sides of the trail. As the trail reaches the end of the tableland, views to the north stretch into the national park and include the North Unit Visitor Center. Leave the state lands after MP 141 and soon begin the descent off the tableland down switchbacks at a self-closing gate. The original MDH was rebuilt here to follow a more sustainable route, but

ABOVE Badlands vista from the Plumely Draw Trailhead.

the descent still is steep, and some gumbo covered areas could be precarious if wet.

Reach the junction with the Summit Trail (N47 33.73, W103 16.966) at MP 142 and a small stock tank surrounded by a triangular fence. The Summit Trail used to lead 4.4 miles east to the Summit Campground on US 85; however, the trail was severely damaged in the wet spring of 2011 by landslides and slumping just south of the largest juniper in North Dakota and was closed by the LMNG, which is reevaluating the status of the trail..

After the Summit Trail junction, enjoy a long, gentle descent crossing a small draw and then following the right bank. Past MP 143, cross a deep wash on a short wooden bridge marked by a yellow caution sign, then turn sharp right to go around a butte with fossilized wood at the base. As of 2020, the DPG plans to begin construction of the less than one-half mile long Sunset Trail that will connect the Maah Daah Hey near MP 143 to the Long X Trail at a point just north on MP 5. At MP 144, the CCC Trail (N47 35.038, W103 16.582) joins from the right providing a 0.3 mile shortcut into the CCC Campground at the end of Loop C. Just beyond, there is a large stainless steel metal post marking the northern end of the Maah Daah Hey. The trail ends at a self-closing gate where the Long X and MDH Trails close their loop (N47 35.182, W103 16.735). The CCC Campground has 38 sites in three loops, vault toilets, and a hand pump for drinking water. The trailhead has a gravel lot, signboard, and register box.

If you have completed the Maah Daah Hey Trail, this is your holy grail. Congratulations on completing one of the longest, and most unique trails, in our country's system of National Grasslands.

ABOVE The original final milepost along the Maah Daah Hey Trail.

3 LITTLE MISSOURI NATIONAL GRASSLAND

The Little Missouri National Grassland (LMNG) is a unique mix of badlands and grassland set in a rugged and remote region. Once home mostly to solitary cattle ranches and isolated oil wells, the LMNG has seen an explosion of interest in recreation. It has responded with a bounty of trails for those seeking experiences ranging from extended expeditions to shorter loop trips.

The Little Missouri National Grassland is part of the Dakota Prairie Grasslands (DPG), managed by the U.S. Department of Agriculture, Forest Service. The DPG has three units in North Dakota and one in northernmost South Dakota. The Sheyenne Ranger District covers 70,000 acres in the eastern part of the state and includes a 31-mile section of the North Country National Scenic Trail and the 7.8-mile Hankinson Hills Trail. The Grand River (155,000 acres in South Dakota) and Cedar River (6,700 acres in North Dakota) straddle the state line and include the 6.7-mile Blacktail Trail. The bulk of the DPG is the 1 million acres of the LMNG, which covers much of the western part of the state. The LMNG is large enough to be split into the northern McKenzie and southern Medora Ranger Districts.

The Forest Service manages national grasslands much like it manages national forests. These are multiple-use areas, and still heavily used for cattle ranching. The western Dakotas contain significant oil and gas fields which are accessed by a maze of gravel roads through otherwise nearly empty country. The construction of the Maah Daah Hey Trail jump started a new emphasis on recreation use

LEFT A golden view of the Little Missouri National Grasslands.
ABOVE A marker along the Summit Trail.

of the grasslands, which has become a popular destination for hikers, mountain bikers, and horseback riders.

DRIVING THE LITTLE MISSOURI NATIONAL GRASSLAND

To navigate the Little Missouri National Grassland, a grasslands map or the most recent Maah Daah Hey Trail map is essential. The most important roads are the Forest Highways, which generally have single digit numbers such as DPG 2. The other main roads have three digit numbers such as DPG 809. Most of these roads are gravel. Many of the roads are surfaced with the distinctive reddish-colored gravel known as "scoria," which is formed from clay that was burned by lignite fires. These roads are generally passable in wet weather. However, roads that lack gravel can be impassable when wet or even damp. In addition to the DPG numbering system, most of the main roads in and around the grasslands are county roads, and others have street addresses such as 140 Street SW. These multiple naming systems can lead to instances where a single piece of road may be known by three different names.

Many road intersections have signs; however, some do not. Also, due to increased oilfield activity, new roads are continually under construction, and even the newest maps are not always up to date. Attention to the map, your direction of travel, and to the car odometer are critical. Be aware that cell phone and internet connections are extremely rare in the backcountry. Motorized vehicles in the LMNG are restricted to existing and marked roads, and are prohibited from trails.

THE TRAIL SYSTEM

Like other national forest units, the Little Missouri National Grassland contains recreation facilities such as campgrounds and picnic areas. However, due to the ease of travel through this open terrain, national grasslands in general have historically lacked developed trail systems. With the development of the Maah Daah Hey Trail, the LMNG has perhaps the best, and largest, trail system of any grassland in the USFS system.

The current trail system in the DPG uses the 144 miles of the Maah Daah Hey Trail as a backbone that almost every trail will eventually connect back to. The second longest trail on the LMNG is the 19-mile Buffalo Gap Trail, a route that was built as a means for mountain bikers to bypass the section of the MDH that passes through the South Unit of Theodore Roosevelt National Park. Buffalo Gap Campground is the center of a cluster of short trails that in turn branch off the Buffalo Gap Trail. Similarly, the Long X and Bennett/ Cottonwood Trails provide loop options and campground access to the north end of the MDH. The Ice Caves Trail provides a link to the Caves and Maah Daah Hey Trail from a dedicated trailhead. The only trail in the LMNG that does not connect to the Maah Daah Hey Trail is the Wolf Trail, located north of the North Unit of Theodore Roosevelt National Park. However, the Wolf Trail was developed to connect the Watford City area to the MDH system through the North Unit of TRNP, and as a first step in going west and south around the North Unit of the TRNP wilderness area on Forest Service lands.

CAMPING AND PICNIC AREAS

In addition to the camping areas constructed along the Maah Daah Hey and Buffalo Gap trails, and described in the Maah Daah Hey chapter, there are two other campgrounds and one picnic area in the Little Missouri National Grassland.

The Summit Campground is located on DPG Road 859 off US 85, just five miles south of the North Unit of Theodore Roosevelt National Park. This campground has three pull-through campsites, two walk-in sites, and picnic shelters. The campground was formerly the trailhead for the now closed Summit Trail and still is the trailhead for the shorter Summit View Trail.

Sather Campground is located in the northwest corner of the grasslands at the junction of ND 16 and ND 68 at Sather Lake Recreation Area. The site has picnic tables, shelters, a pump for potable water, and vault toilets, but no hookups. By the lake, there is a fishing pier and two boat ramps.

Whitetail Picnic Area is located four miles west of Fairfield off US 85 on Whitetail Road. There are ten picnic sites and a vault toilet.

ABOVE Buffalo Gap Viewpoint leads to an interpretive site above the campground.

BUFFALO GAP TRAIL, MEDORA AND MCKENZIE RANGER DISTRICTS

An exciting trail for mountain bikers bypassing the designated Wilderness Area in the South Unit of Theodore Roosevelt National Park.

GENERAL LOCATION: Five miles west of Medora, North Dakota.

HIGHLIGHT: Fun singletrack riding that mixes grasslands and badlands terrain.

ACCESS: There are no facilities at either end of the Buffalo Gap Trail. Many riders start their ride on the Maah Daah Hey Trail at Wannagan Campground (N47 03.335, W103 35.250) which can be reached from I-94 off Exit 23 three miles west of Medora. From Exit 23, turn north on gravel DPG Road 730. At 5.2 miles keep left where a road to the TRNP Petrified Forest Westgate trailhead splits right. At 7.9 miles, cross the Buffalo Gap Trail. At 9.7 miles, turn right onto DPG Road 726, which may not be signed. At 15.8 miles, keep right at the intersection with DPG Road 729. At 16.6 miles, just past the Wannagan trailhead, turn left onto gravel DPG Road 726-15, which leads to the campground at 16.9 miles. The LMNG now asks that day-users park in the new trailhead, rather than the campground, to minimize traffic through the campground. Ride 3.8 miles south to reach the north end of the Buffalo Gap Trail.

The Buffalo Gap trailhead provides easy access to the middle of the trail. To reach the trailhead, take Exit 18 from I-94 west of Medora. Turn north on DPG 726 and then turn left in 0.1 mile and

LEFT Switchbacks along the Maah Daah Hey Trail
ABOVE Grasslands riding offers expansive views.

follow the paved road to reach the Buffalo Gap Campground. The Buffalo Gap Spur and Buffalo Gap Loop trails begin at a trailhead at the north end of the campground. Ride the 1.3-mile Buffalo Gap Spur Trail to reach the Buffalo Gap Trail just north of MP 8.

The south end of the Buffalo Gap Trail is most easily reached from the Maah Daah Hey Trail at 49.3 miles from either the south end at Sully Creek Campground (47.2 miles) or from the crossing of I-94 near Exit 24 (52.5 miles).

DISTANCE: The main trail is 19.0 miles long. The spur to Buffalo Gap Campground is 1.3 miles long. Most riders completing the trail start at Wannagan Creek and ride to Medora for a 27-mile trip.

ALLOWED USES: This trail is open to all non-motorized users, including hikers, mountain bikers, and horseback riders.

MAPS: Little Missouri National Grassland Maah Daah Hey National Recreation Trail 2018, Maah Daah Hey Trail Association Trail Guide (mdhta.com/trail-guide) and Trails Illustrated Theodore Roosevelt National Park (#259); USGS Wannagan Creek East, Wannagan Creek West, Buffalo Gap Campground, and Medora, ND 7.5-minute quadrangles; and Map D.

The Buffalo Gap Trail was completed in 2002 to provide mountain bike riders a route around the designated Wilderness Area in the South Unit of Theodore Roosevelt National Park. Since hikers and horseback riders have access to the more scenic terrain in the national park, it is likely that Buffalo Gap sees far more fat tires than hoof prints or footprints. The Dakota Prairie Grasslands has done an excellent job designing this trail. Though there are few technical sections, only several short pitches are steep enough to cause most riders to walk their bikes. Scenic badlands areas along Wannagan and Andrews creeks are interspersed with fast-paced riding in the trail's middle section. Most of the area is subject to grazing, but riders will also cross three prairie dog towns along the route. Expect a bit of rough riding where the trail may be pockmarked from heavy cattle use.

Because most trail users will be starting on the north end of the trail and riding south into Medora, this trail is described north to south, with the mileposts being counted down, not up. The trail begins at a signed junction with the Maah Daah Hey Trail on the south side of a large stock dam at 61.2 miles, just north of the South Unit of Theodore Roosevelt National Park. To reach this junction from Wannagan Campground, ride 3.8 miles south on the Wannagan and Maah Daah

Hey Trails. The Buffalo Gap Trail is marked with large wooden posts similar to those used on the Maah Daah Hey Trail, but branded with the image of a buffalo skull and the trail name. The DPG added mileposts branded with the Buffalo Gap symbol in 2006. The trail is mostly singletrack and is generally easy to follow except for those inevitable places where it becomes confused with cattle paths.

From the Maah Daah Hey junction at MP 19, turn west and follow the south bank of a small tributary to the main stem of Wannagan Creek. Don't cross the creek, but turn south near a flowing water well at 17.5 miles (N47 01.763, W103 35.250), and enter a large prairie dog town. Be careful not to lose the trail amid myriad cattle paths, and watch for a broad switchback reaching a ridge crest at 16.5 miles. The ridge provides several miles of very scenic riding along the south side of the Wannagan Creek badlands.

The trail leaves the ridge down a steep set of switchbacks to enter rolling grasslands and crosses two small drainages near a pond at 14.2 miles (N47 00.428, W103 36.953). Just as riding across the badlands would be nearly impossible in wet weather, this shadeless section would be unappealing to ride in the full heat of summer. Cross a spur of DPG Road 730 at 12.7 miles, then continue to ride west alongside gravel DPG Road 730 before abruptly turning south and crossing it at 11.7 miles (N47 00.210, W103 39.489). Continue south across the grasslands, cross another unnamed spur road at MP 11, and pass a prairie dog town. Cross one tributary of Knutson Creek at 10.3 miles before crossing the main stem of Kuntson near a pair of signs at 9.3 miles (N46 58.401, W103 39.718). Normally this crossing would be barely enough to wet your tires, but water levels could be higher during spring runoff. A good, solid low water crossing is located between four 4x6 posts, two on each side of the Creek. Beyond Knutson Creek, cross DPG Road 726, then ride alongside it to the signed junction with the Buffalo Gap Spur Trail at 8.3 miles (N46 57.692, W103 39.523). The junction is located immediately north of a second crossing of DPG Road 726.

The Buffalo Gap Spur Trail meanders 1.3 miles to the campground. Facilities here include campsites, potable water, showers, a kiosk, and a gazebo especially welcome to those looking to hide from the sun. The ride back to the junction with the main trail via the paved campground road and gravel DPG Road 726 is 1.4 miles, but probably just as fast as the direct route via the spur. Riders looking for more scenery, less shuttling, and a shorter trip on the Buffalo Gap Trail should start at the campground and ride south into Medora. The DPG has also built the 1.3-mile hard surface Buffalo Gap Loop Trail which leads north across a small wood bridge to a small dam, and the 0.1-mile Buffalo Gap View

Trail (a short hike to the top of a scoria knob within the campground).
The Buffalo Gap Loop Trail is also open to mountain bikes and horses.

From the junction with the spur trail, the main Buffalo Gap Trail
turns east and follows alongside DPG Road 726D past the Buffalo Gap
Ranch. This guest ranch caters to trail users with services including
lodging plus a steakhouse and bar. From the guest ranch, the trail
again turns south past a stock pond at MP 7 and follows a fun, fast
track to a small draw where the trail crosses beneath Interstate 94 in
a wide cattle-sized culvert at 5.6 miles (N46 56.801, W103 37.468).
The I-94 crossing was reconstructed in 2015 to make it safer. Though
some might find this brief trip underground a bit creepy, others will
appreciate a cool break from the unrelenting sun.

Beyond I-94, the Buffalo Gap Trail swings out of sight of the
interstate around a butte and enters the badlands around Andrews Creek.
Enjoy a scenic descent into the valley that crosses Old Highway 10
and goes under the bridge of the Burlington Northern Railroad. Riders
eyeing the railroad should banish any fantasy of converting this line to a
rail trail. If you've ever spent the night in Medora, you know that this is
an active, hard-working railroad. Cross Andrews Creek just south of MP
3 (N46 55.387, W103 35.723). As of 2020, the DPG plans construction of
a low water crossing of Andrews Creek here.

From Andrews Creek, climb to a crossing of gravel DPG Road
745 (West River Road) at 2.6 miles (N46 55.182, W103 35.725). South
of the road ride through another prairie dog town. Enjoy a few more
miles of scenic badlands riding before reaching the end of the Buffalo
Gap Trail at the signed junction with the Maah Daah Hey Trail (N46
54.319, W103 34.235) near mile 49.3 of the Maah Daah Hey. Here the
Maah Daah Hey leads 2.1 miles south to a ford of the Little Missouri
River and Sully Creek State Park, and 5.5 miles to Medora. A drier
option leads north on the Maah Daah Hey 3.2 miles to I-94 and another
1.4 miles east on the paved bike path. Under most conditions, the two
routes will take about, the same time.

RIGHT The trail view approaching the Ice Caves.

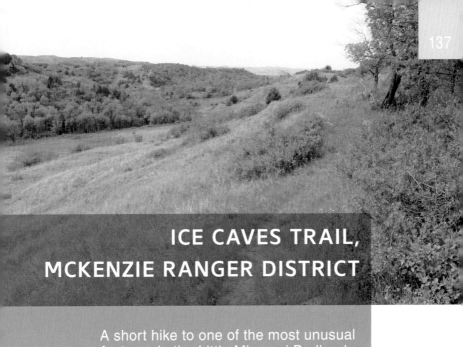

ICE CAVES TRAIL, MCKENZIE RANGER DISTRICT

A short hike to one of the most unusual features in the Little Missouri Badlands.

GENERAL LOCATION: Nine miles southwest of Grassy Butte, North Dakota.

HIGHLIGHT: The Ice Caves.

ACCESS: From US 85, just north of Grassy Butte, turn west onto paved County Road 50, the Beicegal Creek Road. At 6.5 miles, turn left onto gravel DPG 809, the Scairt Woman Road. Just beyond this junction, the Maah Daah Hey Trail crosses the road by the Beicegal Creek Road waterbox. At 9.9 miles, turn left onto DPG 808. At 13.1 miles, keep right where DPG 806 joins from the left. Cross an unsigned two-track road at 13.9 miles, cross the county line, and stay left at the next fork at 14.4 miles. At 14.6 miles, turn right at a trailhead sign onto DPG 713A1 and reach the trailhead at 15.1 miles (N47 19.213, W103 23.678). The trailhead has a gravel parking area, signboard, and register box only.

DISTANCE: The Ice Caves Trail is 1.5 miles long and the caves can be reached in one mile. The 3-mile roundtrip hike to the end of the trail at the Maah Daah Hey Trail intersection can include a return trip on the Aspen Trail. Also, mountain bikers can ride the Ice Caves and Maah Daah Hey Trails to the north plus part of the gravel access roads to form either a 13.7 or 20.7 mile loop.

ALLOWED USES: This trail is open to all non-motorized users, including hikers, mountain bikers, and horseback riders.

MAPS: Little Missouri National Grassland Maah Daah
Hey National Recreation Trail 2018, Maah Daah Hey Trail
Association Trail Guide (mdhta.com/trail-guide), and Trails
Illustrated Theodore Roosevelt National Park (#259), and USGS
Squaretop Butte, ND 7.5-minute quadrangle and Map D.

The Ice Caves are the most unusual formation in a region known for its
bizarre and broken topography. Their location well off the beaten path
and accessibility only by miles of gravel road ensures that the caves
remain little visited. The Ice Caves are not like typical caves that may
form by dissolution of limestone or by volcanic activity. The ridge to
the north of and above the caves is formed by a sandstone layer that is
exceptionally thick by badlands standards. As the ridge weathered over
time, the sandstone eroded with large blocks breaking off and falling to
the valley below. Between the large fallen blocks are large open spaces
that remain as the blocks pile atop one another. As the stack of blocks

ABOVE The Ice Caves are one of the most unusual features of the
Little Missouri National Grassland.

grew, some of these spaces remain open as caves. During the winter the spaces become filled with snow that can compact into ice, but even in summer they are insulated from the heat by the rocks above them. While the caves now only rarely contain ice in summer, they will remain a cool treat for visitors.

The Ice Caves Trail begins by following the trailhead road west, and then soon branches off to the left side down a wide gully. The trail is marked by the LMNG's familiar large wooden posts, branded with the Ice Caves' snowflake logo. At 0.7 mile (N47 18.949, W103 24.185), reach the junction with the Aspen Trail which splits left. The Aspen Trail loops south and reconnects with the Ice Caves Trail in 0.3 mile after a traverse through a grove of its namesake trees, and makes a fine return route for hikers heading all the way out to the Maah Daah Hey Trail.

Stay right at the Aspen Trail junction to reach the Ice Caves. There are no signs to guide you to the individual caves, but user paths mark the routes to many of the openings. Watch for the cool openings among the jumbled boulders, but also keep an eye on the high cliffs above you where the boulders were shed from. At 1.0 mile, leave the caves and reach the signed junction with the far end of the Aspen Trail (N47 18.895, W103 24.461).

Beyond the Aspen Trail junction, descend through some badlands, follow a creek bed, and then cross another draw to reach the end of the Ice Caves Trail at a junction with the Maah Daah Hey Trail at 1.5 miles (N47 18.911, W103 25.010). The junction is 108.6 miles on the Maah Daah Hey Trail and, from there, 3.3 miles south to the Magpie Trail junction and 18.8 miles north to the Bennett Trail junction.

For mountain bikers, there are two potential loop trips that can be made using the Ice Caves Trail and the Maah Daah Hey Trail to the north. The short loop starts by riding Ice Caves Trail to the MDH junction and going 6.3 miles north on the MDH to the crossing of DPG 809. Then turn right and ride 0.7 mile east to the junction of DPG 809 and 808 at the 9.9 mile mark of the drive to the trailhead. Then ride back to the trailhead for a 13.7 mile loop. For the longer loop, continue north on the Maah Daah Hey Trail past the first crossing of DPG 809 to the second crossing located just past Hanson Overlook near the Beicegal Creek Road waterbox and just short of County Road 50. Turn right here and ride south on the trailhead access route to complete a 20.7 mile loop.

IN MEMORY
OF
BENNETT JAY
KRYZSKO
1968-2000
2003

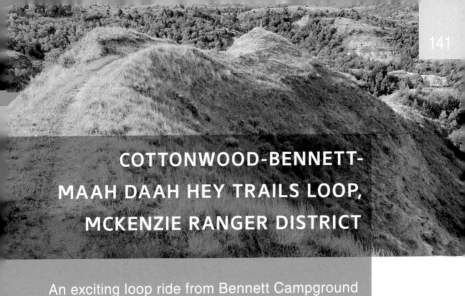

COTTONWOOD-BENNETT-MAAH DAAH HEY TRAILS LOOP, MCKENZIE RANGER DISTRICT

An exciting loop ride from Bennett Campground that combines the Cottonwood and Bennett trails with the Maah Daah Hey Trail.

GENERAL LOCATION: Eight miles northwest of Grassy Butte, North Dakota.

HIGHLIGHT: Long sections of relatively smooth riding combines with plenty of badlands scenery.

ACCESS: From US 85 7.5 miles north of Grassy Butte, turn west onto the gravel Bennett Creek Road (aka 6th Street NW) at a sign for the Bennett Campground. At 4.0 miles, turn left onto signed DPG 824. At 4.5 miles, turn right onto DPG 824-4 at a sign for the campground. Reach the Bennett trailhead at 5.3 miles. There is gravel parking at the Bennett trailhead with a signboard and register box. The Bennett Campground (N47 29.444, W103 21.083) has 13 sites, a hand pump for drinking water, and is accessible off a spur of the Bennett Trail. This loop can also be accessed from the south via County Road 50, the Beicegel Creek Road at 120.1 miles on the MDH, or at DPG 809 at 119.2 miles. However, there is no parking area on County 50, so that stopping near the Beicegal Creek Road waterbox on DPG 809 may be the best option.

DISTANCE: The loop is 15.1 miles long. Many riders will also want to include a side trip to the China Wall which adds another 2.6 miles roundtrip. Access via paved County Road 50 would add an additional 4.6 miles roundtrip.

LEFT Bennett Trail commemorative marker.
ABOVE Idyllic ridge-top riding on the Cottonwood Trail.

ALLOWED USES: This trail is open to all non-motorized users, including hikers, mountain bikers, and horseback riders.

MAPS: Little Missouri National Grassland Maah Daah Hey National Recreation Trail 2018, Maah Daah Hey Trail Association Trail Guide (mdhta.com/trail-guide), and Trails Illustrated Theodore Roosevelt National Park (#259), USGS Buckskin Butte and Wolf Coulee, ND 7.5-minute quadrangles and Map D.

The Bennett and Cottonwood trails offer one of the few opportunities to ride a singletrack loop using the Maah Daah Hey Trail. The ease of access to the trailhead off US 85 makes this a popular area to visit, and a short side trip to the China Wall puts some icing on the cake.

From the trailhead (N47 29.502, W103 21.140), the Bennett Trail is almost immediately joined on the left by a spur trail leading to the campground. The trail heads south, drops to a self-closing gate, and then makes a normally dry crossing of Bennett Creek. A good, solid low water crossing was constructed in 2005. Across the creek at 0.3 mile is the signed junction (N47 29.362, W103 21.182) with the Cottonwood Trail, which splits to the left. On the right is the Bennett Trail, which will be your return route. The junction is near what should be MP 7 for the Cottonwood Trail. The Cottonwood Trail was built in 2005 and substantially repaired after damage from the extremely wet spring of 2011. All three trails are marked by a well-defined tread and the large wooden posts used by the LMNG branded with the MDH turtle, the Cottonwood leaf, and Bennett ram icons. To follow the loop clockwise, turn left onto the Cottonwood Trail.

The climb from the Cottonwood junction to the butte above it is less than 400 feet, but don't be surprised if some pushing up the switchbacks is needed. The climb is the toughest part of the entire ride, and the trails ahead are much less steep. Reach MP 6 just before reaching the top of the butte and starting a well-deserved gentle ride across the grassland. MP 5 is found just before a gate. Continue along the ridgetop passing occasional small groves of aspen and looping around the head of a tributary of Cottonwood Creek.

Cross a self-closing gate shortly before reaching MP 4 (N47 27.848, W103 21.071). From MP 4, descend to pass above the head of a dry wash, cross a self-closing gate, and then traverse east along a shaded section of trail. After MP 3, climb on long switchbacks up a shaded north slope. After another stretch of level riding, descend through some badlands on the west side of a small butte where some slump blocks are found.

Descend from MP 2, cross another gate, and reach the signed crossing of Cottonwood Creek at 1.3 miles (N47 26.881, W103 20.595). The Cottonwood crossing can be muddy even when the rest of the trail is dry. At MP 1, begin the climb from Cottonwood Creek using switchbacks in a wooded section, then enjoy some fast riding across the grassland to the "T" intersection with the Maah Daah Hey Trail at 122.4 miles (N47 26.605, W103 21.487). You are now seven miles into the loop. The Maah Daah Hey Trail leads left 2.3 miles to paved County Road 50 (N47 25.170, W103 21.878) at 120.1 miles.

Bear right at the junction to turn onto the Maah Daah Hey Trail heading north and to continue to follow the loop clockwise. Pass a stock tank while following the narrow extension of the tableland to the north on some fun, fast riding. To the east is Cottonwood Creek. Enjoy some good creek views before dropping off the north end of the tableland on some switchbacks. Pass another stock tank before crossing the usually dry west fork of Cottonwood Creek at MP 124 (N47 27.599, W103 22.118). The Maah Daah Hey Trail then follows the west bank of the creek and across several small coulees.

Cross through a self-closing gate at 124.5 miles, which may mark the upper limit of water in Cottonwood Creek. On the next small divide is a petrified wood locality, which also offers some broader vistas. Next, pass another small pond before turning up a side coulee at 125.5 miles to avoid crossing the very deep canyon of another west fork of Cottonwood Creek. The DPG plans a minor reroute here to improve this crossing. The trail continues north along Cottonwood Creek. Then the terrain turns

ABOVE Scenery along the Cottonwood Trail

monotonously flat and is covered in dense sagebrush. At 126.7 miles, cross the dry bed of another Cottonwood Creek tributary.

Reach the signed junction with the Bennett Trail at 127.4 miles (N47 29.578, W103 23.687) just before leaving Cottonwood Creek to the west near the confluence with Bennett Creek and another petrified wood locality. You are now 12 miles into the loop. If you would like to visit the China Wall, keep left here on the Maah Daah Hey Trail and ride 1.3 miles to the top of the wall.

To continue on the loop and return to Bennett Campground, turn right at the junction. You will now count up on the mileposts for the Bennett Creek Trail. Cross Cottonwood Creek at 0.2 mile. If the creek bottom looks too wet, a drier crossing may be found upstream. Beyond the crossing, enjoy some easy riding on a grass and sagebrush covered bench on the south side of Bennett Creek. At 1.3 miles, ride down to Bennett Creek at the mouth of a draw entering from the south, but do not cross Bennett Creek here. At 1.6 miles, there is a sharp right turn by a sink hole that formed in 2019. Just before MP 2 is a trail marker dedicated to the memory of Bennett Jay Kryzsko.

At 2.8 miles, close the loop at the junction with the Cottonwood Trail (N47 29.362, W103 21.182). Turn left here and recross Bennett Creek to return to the trailhead. If you take the right fork of the trail into the campground, you will pass MP 3 before reaching the start of the campground loop at 3.1 miles.

ABOVE Sign marking the junction of the Maah Daah Hey and Cottonwood trails.
RIGHT Rugged badlands approaching the Little Missouri River.

LONG X-MAAH DAAH HEY TRAIL LOOP, MCKENZIE RANGER DISTRICT

A great mix of badlands and grassland riding in the shadow of the North Unit of Theodore Roosevelt National Park.

GENERAL LOCATION: Fifteen miles south of Watford City, North Dakota.

HIGHLIGHT: An excellent mix of rugged badlands scenery and easy grasslands riding.

ACCESS: From US 85 just 0.8 mile south of the Theodore Roosevelt National Park North Unit entrance and immediately south of the bridge over the Little Missouri River, turn west onto DPG 842 at signs for the Little Missouri National Grassland CCC Campground. Stay right at a cattle guard at 0.9 mile and enter the campground at 1.1 miles. Pass the starts of loops C (left), A (right), and B (left) to reach the Maah Daah Hey trailhead (N47 35.182, W103 16.735) at 1.3 miles. The trailhead has a gravel parking area, signboard, and register box. The campground has 38 camp sites, a picnic shelter, latrines, and a hand pump for drinking water. The CCC Trail (N47 35.113, W103 16.389) leaves from the end of loop C at a trail register by a signpost and self-closing gate to connect to the MDH in 0.3 mile at MP 144.

DISTANCE: The loop is 11.3 miles long.

ALLOWED USES: This trail is open to all non-motorized users, including hikers, mountain bikers, and horseback riders.

MAPS: Little Missouri National Grassland Maah Daah Hey National Recreation Trail 2018, Maah Daah Hey Trail Association Trail Guide (mdhta.com/trail-guide), Trails Illustrated Theodore Roosevelt National Park (#259), USGS Long X Divide, ND 7.5-minute quadrangle, and Map D.

The Long X Trail combines with the northern end of the Maah Daah Hey Trail (MDH) to form one of the most interesting and scenic loops in the North Dakota badlands. The northern half of the trail passes through rugged badlands with views of the Little Missouri River and of the North Unit of Theodore Roosevelt National Park. The south half of the loop traverses over high, lonesome grasslands and is more reminiscent of the heyday of cattle ranching in the region.

The Long X Trail commemorates one of the major routes used in the 1800s era cattle drives to the North Dakota badlands. The route roughly followed what is now US 85 from the Wyoming side of the Black Hills to the head of the Little Missouri River and then to the badlands. The Long X Ranch was operated by the Reynolds brothers from Texas and located at the north end of Squaw Creek near the North Unit of Theodore Roosevelt National Park. The cattle were typically grazed for two years then driven to Medora and shipped to markets by rail. The Long X Ranch was located in what is now the North Unit of TRNP. Like so many other operations, it was closed after the devastating winter of 1886-87.

The Long X Trail shares a trailhead with the northern end of the Maah Daah Hey Trail at the CCC Campground. The trails start immediately beyond a self-closing gate at the far south end of the trailhead parking area. To travel the Long X Trail first and follow the loop counterclockwise, take the right fork which will take you alongside the Little Missouri River. You will be counting down on the mileposts on the Long X Trail. Both the Long X and Maah Daah Hey Trails here have well-defined treads, and both are marked with large wooden trail posts; those for the MDH have the familiar turtle symbol, while the Long X posts, not surprisingly, are branded with "Long X."

At 0.3 mile, pass a short side-trail leading to Homers Camp, which offers a grassy campsite and picnic table on the bank of the Little Missouri River. The camp was named for Homer Paintner who maintained the camp for decades as a Forest Service employee, mostly on his own time. Generations of people used the camp for picnics, celebrations, and camping before the access road finally deteriorated enough to prevent vehicle access. The trail then heads up the valley of a small draw. Near the head of the draw the cattle tend to bear left while the trail turns right. At 0.7 mile, cross a small creek. Since you are travelling the Long X Trail in the reverse direction, the first mile marker encountered is MP 5. As of 2020, the DPG plans to begin construction of the less than one half mile long Sunset Trail that will connect the Maah Daah Hey near MP 143 to the Long X Trail at a point just north on MP 5. Enjoy some river views and the shade from scattered juniper trees as you ride through the grassland.

At 1.5 miles, cross another dry wash by a very wide fossilized tree stump. The trail beyond this point enters some rugged badlands. At 1.8 miles, reach MP 4 (N47 34.400, W103 17.924). Cross two more dry washes as the trail continues west above the valley of the Little Missouri. Beyond the second wash, the trail turns south and away from the river. After MP 3, the climb from the river gets more serious with some shaded switchbacks gradually yielding to a gentler climb through grassland.

Reach the rim of the upper grassland at 3.5 miles and cross a self-closing gate near the top. At 3.8 miles, reach MP 2 (N47 34.077, W103 19.407), and at 4.0 miles, turn left onto an old two-track road. The two-track road will bend left by an old stock tank. Just before reaching MP 1, the trail veers left off the two-track to drop into a small draw which offers a badly needed patch of shade. From here, follow the posts back to the two-track road. At 5.8 miles, reach the junction with the Maah Daah Hey Trail at its 138.8 miles (N47 32.724, W103 19.393) near a fence corner.

From the fence corner, DPG Road 825 bears right; there is a waterbox at the junction. The Maah Daah Hey Trail continues straight ahead to the east. MP 139 is within sight ahead, and a welcome patch of shade lies just beyond. The trail soon parallels the two-track road and follows it to the northeast across the sunny tableland. After entering state lands, the trail moves west of the two-track road briefly, rejoins it, then passes a stock tank. Near MP 140, a stock tank and pond lie on opposite sides of the trail. As the trail reaches the end of the tableland, views to the north stretch into the national park and include the North Unit Visitor Center. Leave the state lands after MP 141 and soon afterward begin the descent off the tableland down switchbacks at a self-closing gate. The original Maah Daah Hey Trail was rebuilt here to follow a more sustainable route, but the descent is still steep, and some gumbo covered areas could be precarious if wet.

Reach a junction with the now closed Summit Trail (N47 33.73, W103 16.966) at MP 142 and a small stock tank surrounded by a triangular fence. The Summit Trail led 4.4 miles east to the Summit Campground on US 85 across some of the most spectacular badlands on the LMNG. However, the Summit Trail was badly damaged by slumping in the wet spring of 2011 and has not been repaired. The

Little Missouri National Grassland considers the trail closed, but will be reevaluating the status of the trail in 2020.

After the Summit Trail junction, enjoy a long gentle descent crossing a small draw and then following the right bank. Past MP 143, cross a deep wash on a short wooden bridge marked by a yellow caution sign, then turn sharp right to go around a butte with fossilized wood at the base. At MP 144, the CCC Trail (N47 35.038, W103 16.582) joins from the right providing a 0.3 mile shortcut into the CCC Campground at the end of Loop C. Just beyond, there is a large stainless steel post marking the northern end of the Maah Daah Hey Trail. The trail ends at a self-closing gate where the Long X and Maah Daah Hey Trails close their loop (N47 35.182, W103 16.735). The CCC Campground has 38 sites in three loops and a hand pump for drinking water. Loop B is closed to horses. The trailhead has a gravel lot, signboard, and register box. The CCC Trail leaves from the end of loop C at a trail register by a signpost and swing gate. From the campground, it descends to cross a small draw, then joins the Maah Daah Hey Trail at MP 144 in 0.3 mile (N47 35.638, W103 16.582).

ABOVE A spur trail leads from the Maah Daah Hey to the CCC Campground.
RIGHT Sagebrush and Prairie Smoke.

OTHER LITTLE MISSOURI NATIONAL GRASSLANDS TRAILS

JUNIPER SPUR TRAIL The 0.1-mile *Juniper Spur Trail* leads to a viewing point south of the Burning Coal Vein Campground. From the Maah Daah Hey trailhead in the campground (N46 35.611, W103 26.502), go 0.5 mile south to the end of the road to the unmarked trailhead and hike to the far end of a small butte which has expansive views south toward Amidon (N46 35.527, W103 26.416). Be careful descending the steps from the trailhead down to the area of the columnar junipers.

MAAH DAAH HEY CONNECTING TRAILS Several short trails branch off the Maah Daah Hey Trail and are described in more detail in the Maah Daah Hey Trail chapter. From south to north, the Bear Creek, (0.3 mile), Coal Creek (0.7 mile), Coal Creek Spur (0.1 mile), Survey Monument (0.15 mile), Bully Pulpit (0.2 mile), Wannagan (0.2 mile), Wannagan Spur (0.2 mile), Elkhorn (0.3 mile), Magpie (0.4 mile), and CCC (0.3 mile) trails all lead from the Maah Daah Hey to their respective campgrounds or trailheads.

BUFFALO GAP CAMPGROUND TRAILS The *Buffalo Gap Campground* is the epicenter for a network of similarly named trails that connect to the Maah Daah Hey Trail. The main Buffalo Gap Trail is a 19-mile trail that connects to the Maah Daah Hey Trail and provides a bypass trail for mountain bikes around the designated Wilderness Area in the South Unit of Theodore Roosevelt National Park. The Buffalo Gap Trail is described in detail above. The 1.3-mile Buffalo Gap Spur Trail connects the campground to the main Buffalo Gap Trail just north of MP 8 and the crossing of DPG 726. The Buffalo Gap Spur Trail shares the first 0.4 mile of the Buffalo Gap Loop Trail. The Buffalo Gap Loop Trail is a

1.8-mile hard-surface trail loop open to nonmotorized use that starts at the campground and circles a large pond to the north. Adding to the confusion of similarly named trails is the 0.1-mile Buffalo Gap Viewpoint Trail, which starts off the campground road to the east of the campground and leads to a vista on a scoria knob. To reach the Buffalo Gap Campground take Exit 18 off Interstate 94 and go north on paved DPG 726. After 0.1 mile from the bottom of the exit ramp, turn left to pass the Viewpoint Trail at 0.3 mile and reach the trailhead at 0.7 mile. The campground has 37 sites, flush toilets, pay showers, a large gazebo, and a wash hose for muddy bikes and bikers. Camping is first come, first served.

ASPEN TRAIL

The 0.3-mile *Aspen Trail* forms a short loop with the Ice Caves Trail and is described in more detail above.

HANSON OVERLOOK

The Little Missouri National Grassland added a short connector trail from the Maah Daah Hey Trail to *Hanson Overlook* just south of MP 119 in the fall of 2019. The new trail is less than 0.1 mile long and replaces user-created trails that were causing erosion on the steep slope up to the Overlook. At the overlook, there is a bench and an informational panel complete with old pictures of the Hanson family and the old Hanson Family Ranch site.

SUMMIT AND SUMMIT VIEW TRAILS

The 4.4 mile *Summit Trail* was rebuilt in the 2007 and then closed because of slumping damage from the extremely wet spring of 2011. The trail connected the LMNG Summit Campground with the Maah Daah Hey Trail at MP 142. The trail is now closed, but the LMNG will reevaluate its status in 2020. The Summit Campground is located off US 85 just south of the North Unit of Theodore Roosevelt National Park.

ABOVE Flowers of the Downy Paintbrush appear in June and July.

Also, near the Summit Campground is the 0.2 mile *Summit Viewpoint Trail* (LMNG Trail #8017), which, not surprisingly, leads to a good overlook.

SUNSET TRAIL As of 2020 the DPG plans to begin construction of the less than one half mile long Sunset Trail that will connect the Maah Daah Hey near MP 143 to the Long X Trail at a point just north on MP 5.

WOLF TRAIL The 8.75 mile *Wolf Trail* is the newest addition to the Little Missouri National Grassland system and was completed in 2011. Unlike other trails in the system, the Wolf Trail stands alone and doesn't connect to the Maah Daah Hey or other Forest Service trails. The Wolf Trail is located north of the North Unit of Theodore Roosevelt National Park and provides a grassland walk through rolling terrain. The trail ends at the western boundary of the North Unit and is marked by posts with a wolf print brand. This trail was developed to connect the Watford City area to the MDH system on the road through the North Unit of Theodore Roosevelt National Park. In 2019, US 85 was being upgraded to a four-lane highway and the plans included a trail alongside the road from Watford City to the Long X bridge for future trail users.

To reach the Wolf trailhead from US 85, drive 4.0 miles south from Watford City, or 10.5 miles north from the North Unit of Theodore Roosevelt National Park, and turn west onto County Road 30. In 4.0 miles, the road turns south to become 130th Avenue SE. In another 3.0 miles, the road turns west and becomes 220th Street NW. Make a left turn in another 0.5 mile onto dirt 130 M Ave NW. The trailhead is two miles south at the end of the road.

ABOVE Purple vetch along the Summit Trail.

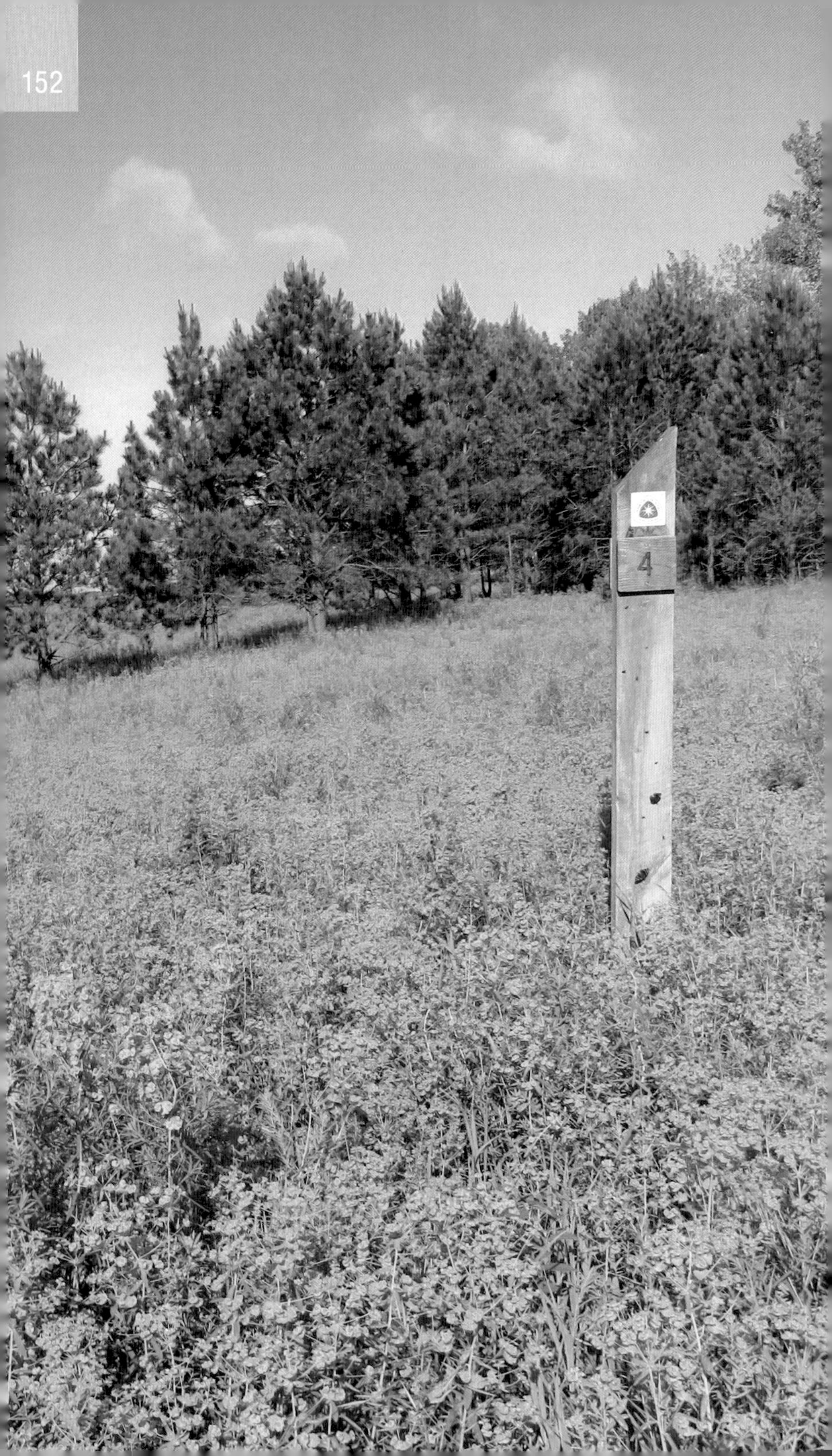
4

4 NORTH COUNTRY NATIONAL SCENIC TRAIL & THE SHEYENNE NATIONAL GRASSLAND

Extending the range of this guidebook is the North Dakota segment of the North Country National Scenic Trail (NCNST). The North Country Trail is the second longest in the grasslands and easily warrants stretching some boundaries. Like the more famous Appalachian and Pacific Crest national scenic trails, the North Country Trail has been designated by Congress, is administered by the National Park Service, and is designed to provide national caliber recreation opportunities. The North Country Trail is envisioned as a 4,600-mile trail leading through seven states from Lake Champlain near Crown Point State Historic Site in New York to Lake Sakakawea State Park near the Garrison Dam on the Missouri River in North Dakota. Here the North Country Trail ends where it joins the route of the Lewis and Clark National Historic Trail. The final 430 miles of the trail is in North Dakota. The North Country Trail was conceived in the 1970s and designated by Congress in 1980. Trail construction has been steady, but slow since then. Over 1,900 trail miles have been built and certified. One obstacle for the trail builders and designers is the lack of public lands for the trail corridor across much of the proposed route. This problem is especially acute across eastern and central North Dakota where there is very little public land.

Luckily for North Dakotans, there is a 31-mile section of the trail in place in the 70,000 acre Sheyenne National Grassland, just east of Lisbon in the southeast corner of the state. Here the trail wanders through grasslands far more heavily used by cattle than humans. The

LEFT Leafy spurge has invaded much of the Sheyenne National Grassland.
ABOVE A self-closing gate in the Sheyenne National Grassland.

trail was resurfaced with compacted gravel between the east and west trailhead in 2005 to offer an all-weather trail, and it is marked by the DPG's branded wooden posts. Trail users will find both artesian wells (with a high concentration of dissolved minerals) and windmill-powered wells (summer only) that deliver non-potable water for cattle. The Sheyenne National Grassland also installed self-closing gates across the cattle fences in 2005.

The 31 miles of trail in the Sheyenne National Grassland is easily accessible. There are trailheads at the west end (MP 0), middle (MP 15), and near Jorgen's Hollow Campground (MP 28) near the east end. Jorgen's Hollow Campground has 14 primitive campsites, seven of these allow horses. There are two vault toilets and a hand pump for potable water. Occupancy is first-come, first-served. The Oak Leaf Trail also starts from the campground and forms a four-mile loop with the North Country Trail.

Motorized vehicles are not allowed on the trail, but the trail is open to horses and mountain bikes. Leave No Trace camping is permitted anywhere on the grasslands, except at trailheads. Due to the lack of firewood, camp stoves are essential. Hunting (white-tail deer and turkey) and fishing are also popular uses of this area.

LEFT The Sheyenne River in Fort Ransom State Park.
ABOVE Sturdy wooden posts mark the North Country Trail.

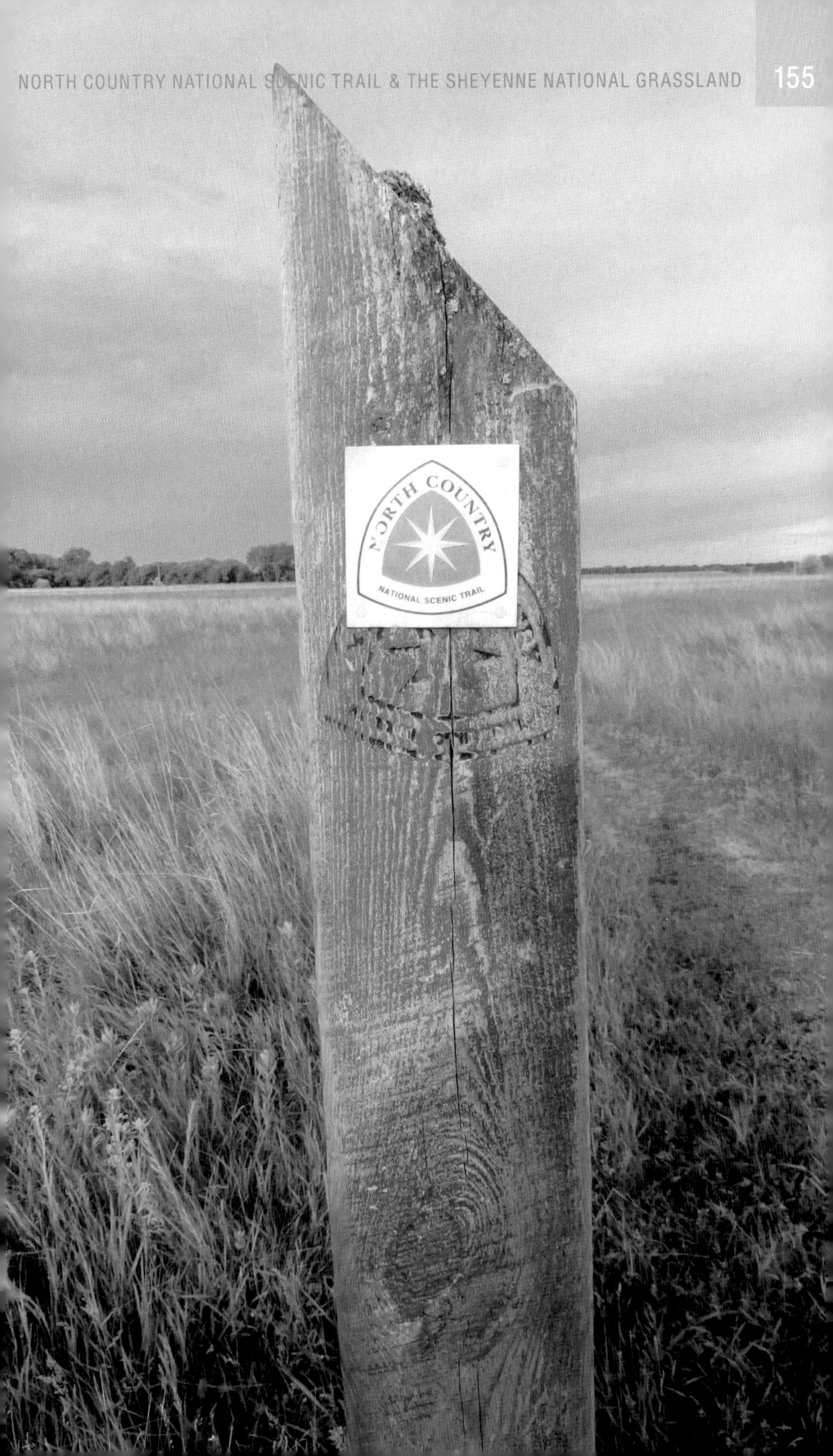
NORTH COUNTRY
NATIONAL SCENIC TRAIL

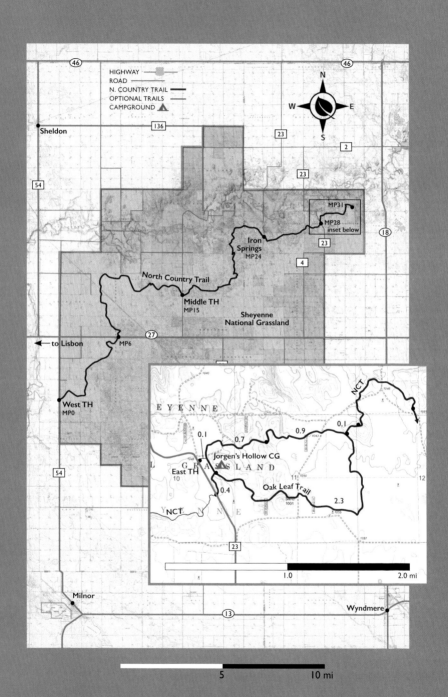

HIGHWAY
ROAD
N. COUNTRY TRAIL
OPTIONAL TRAILS
CAMPGROUND

N
W   E
S

Sheldon

MP31

MP28
inset below

Iron
Springs
MP24

North Country Trail

Middle TH
MP15

Sheyenne
National Grassland

to Lisbon

MP6

West TH
MP0

CHEYENNE

NCT

0.1   0.7   0.9   0.1

Jorgen's Hollow CG

East TH

0.4   Oak Leaf Trail

2.3

NCT

GRASSLAND

1.0   2.0 mi

Milnor

Wyndmere

5   10 mi

NORTH COUNTRY NATIONAL SCENIC TRAIL, SOUTHWEST SECTION, SHEYENNE RANGER DISTRICT

An easy ride across mixed grassland for mountain bikers, horseback riders, and hikers.

GENERAL LOCATION: Thirteen miles southeast of Lisbon, North Dakota.

HIGHLIGHT: Fun riding across a level prairie dotted with groves of bur oak.

ACCESS: From Lisbon, drive ten miles east on ND 27 to the junction with Ransom County 54, which is also 141st Av. SE. Drive three miles south to the signed West trailhead for the North Country Trail on the left (N46 23.936, W97 28.130). The trailhead has a gravel parking area, signboard, and trail register. There is no designated parking area at the far end where the North Country Trail crosses ND 27 at the turnaround for this trip.

DISTANCE: This segment is 12.2 miles roundtrip.

ALLOWED USES: This trail is open to all non-motorized users, including hikers, mountain bikers, and horseback riders.

MAPS: Sheyenne National Grassland North Country and Oak Leaf Trails, USGS Venlo, ND quadrangle, and Map E.

ABOVE Along the North Country Trail.

For hikers used to mountain trails or those across the rugged badlands, the Sheyenne National Grassland trails provide a major change of scenery. Here the land is nearly flat, but the views still extend far into the distance. The wildflowers share some similarities with those of the west, but new species are also filling these new habitats. Like the badlands, the oak savanna here is sparsely forested, exposing travelers to the full effects of sun, rain, or wind.

At the West trailhead there is a large survey control monument celebrating 100 years of the US Forest Service (N46 23.936, W97 28.130). From here, head northeast across the grassland on the North Country Trail. All of this trail section can be used for grazing, so please avoid spooking any cattle and be sure to leave any gates that you encounter as you find them. At 0.4 mile, you cross your first self-closing gate through a fence separating two pastures. At 0.7 mile, cross a long wooden boardwalk over a marshy section of trail. Despite cattle grazing and a nearly flat profile, the trail tread here is in remarkably good shape and should greatly appeal to mountain bike riders looking for some easy cruising. Much of the NCT has been surfaced with the application of 4 inches of compacted gravel.

The North Country Trail is marked by a well-defined footpath, with some minor exceptions where cattle congregate near gates, and by the large wooden posts similar to those used to mark the Maah Daah Hey Trail. Some posts are labelled with a North Country Trail brand and others have a blue NCT symbol attached. There are also mileposts, and MP 1 shows up right on schedule after the second self-closing gate.

Pass one more self-closing gate before the trail turns north and pass a stock tank to reach MP 2 (N46 24.485, W97 26.489). Be careful at the next gate where there is an electrified fence and it crosses an old ranch two-track road at 2.6 miles. There is a self-closing gate at 3.4 miles and another just before MP 4 (N46 25.618, W97 25.451). The wooded area here is only one quarter of a mile long, but summer visitors especially will cherish the only patch of shade available on this trip. The woods are pine, juniper, and oak and the occasional linear alignment of the trees indicate that these woods may have been planted as a windbreak.

Just after the four-mile woods, cross two more gates and then cross a faint two-track road. You'll recross this road at a gate between a corral and a small windmill just before reaching MP 5. Follow the two-track road for one quarter of a mile before turning sharply right. At 5.4 miles, reach a gate, and at 5.7 miles turn sharply left to head north toward ND 27. Cross a short wooden bridge over a muddy area before reaching MP 6. After crossing through your last gate, reach the end of the hike at ND 27 by a paved pullout at 6.1 miles (N46 26.513,

W97 24.392). The North Country Trail continues directly across the road on an old two-track road but there is no designated trailhead at this crossing of ND 27.

The Sheyenne National Grassland is an excellent birding area. It is North Dakota's only home of the greater prairie chicken. April is the best month to view these birds as the males display to attract females. Migratory songbirds such as warblers, vireos, meadowlarks, bluebirds, and orioles abound in the spring. The most abundant species surveyed on the grassland are various hawks, grasshopper sparrow, red-winged blackbird, clay-colored sparrow, savannah sparrow, and common yellowthroat.

ABOVE Butte Candle is an early spring bloomer.

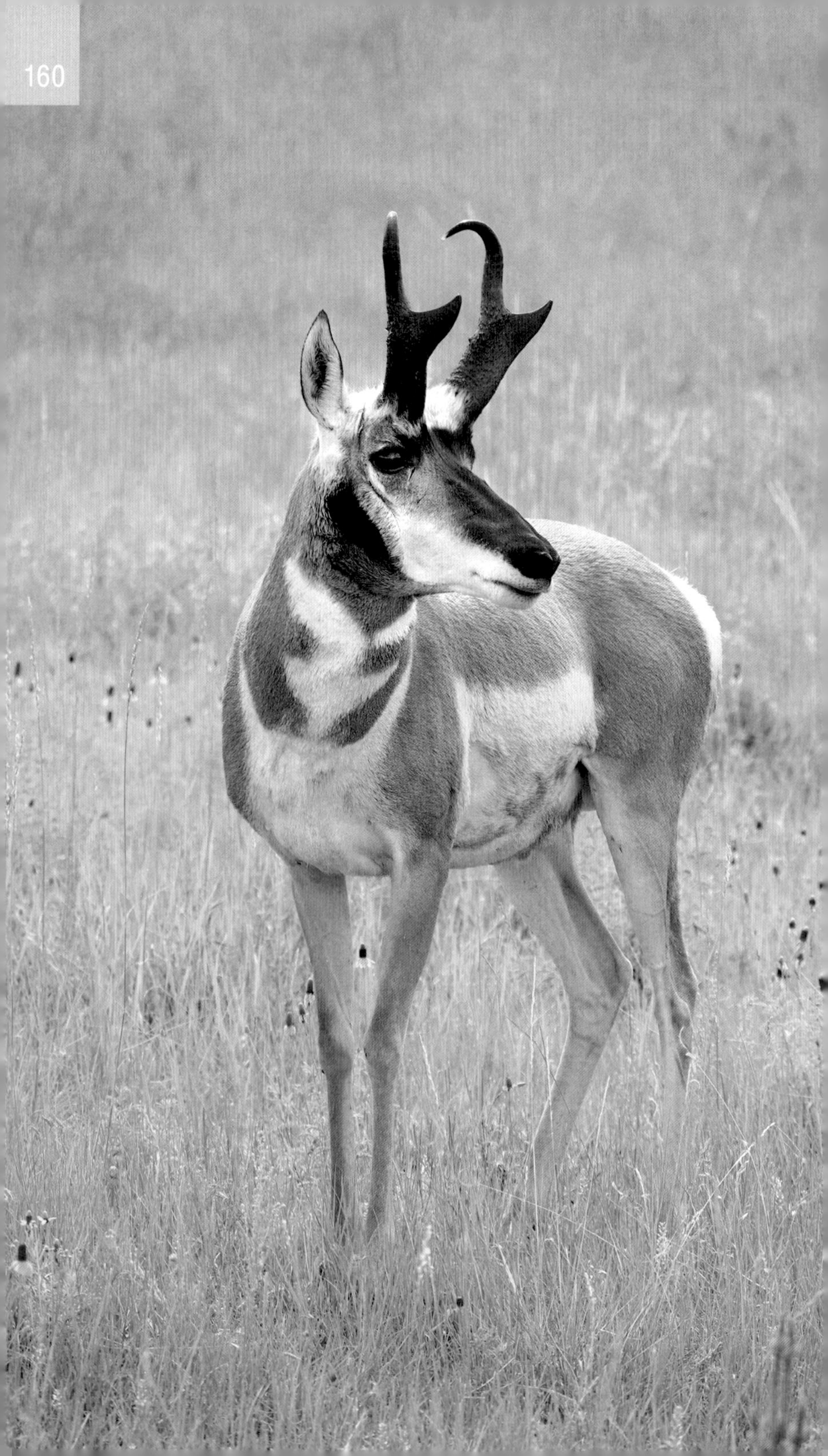

NORTH COUNTRY NATIONAL SCENIC TRAIL, IRON SPRINGS CREEK SECTION, SHEYENNE RANGER DISTRICT

A beautiful introduction to the Sheyenne National Grassland and the North Country Trail.

GENERAL LOCATION: 19 miles north of Wyndmere, North Dakota.

HIGHLIGHT: Oak savannah and tallgrass prairie.

ACCESS: To access the east trailhead from the junction of state highways 18 and 46 just south of the community of Leonard, drive south for five miles on paved County Road 23. Next turn left and drive east one mile on gravel County Road 2. Then turn right onto gravel County 23 and drive south four miles to the signed trailhead (N46 31.383, W97 12.175) near the Jorgen's Hollow Campground. Or, from the town of Lisbon, drive 22 miles east on ND 27 to the junction with gravel County Road 4. Turn left and drive north to a signed junction with County Road 23 at 26 miles. At 28.7 miles, reach the North Country trailhead on the right. The trailhead has a gravel parking area, signboard, and register box.

DISTANCE: This segment is 8.4 miles round trip.

ALLOWED USES: This trail is open to all non-motorized users, including hikers, mountain bikers, and horseback riders.

MAPS: Sheyenne National Grassland North Country and Oak Leaf Trails, USGS Coburn and Power, ND quadrangles, and Map E.

LEFT A pronghorn enjoying the summer grass.
ABOVE Approaching the Four Mile Wood.

The Sheyenne National Grassland (SNG) is home to one of the longest and most scenic sections of the North Country National Scenic Trail in North Dakota. The diverse scenery and prolific bird life on the Iron Springs Section make this an excellent introduction to hiking on the grassland. The soil of the grasslands was formed from a thick mantle of sand deposited by advancing glaciers. The northern end of the grassland is oak savanna, a gentle prairie dotted with groves of bur oak. Along the Sheyenne River are hardwood forests of basswood, American elm, and green ash.

The North Country Trail (NCT) in the Sheyenne Grassland was completely rebuilt in 2005. Though the rebuild included a major reroute to avoid marshy areas, some low-lying sections of the trail can still be boggy in wet weather. Muddy areas in the first 0.4 mile of the trail can be bypassed by using lightly used County Road 23. The trail tread was surfaced with gravel to prevent damage from the horse traffic the trail receives, and to protect the tread from wind erosion. The trail is marked by carsonite posts and the tall wooden posts branded with the North Country Trail North Star symbol. Mileposts along the trail are numbered west to east, opposite the direction of this description. Except for a few sandy areas and some steep sections damaged by horse traffic, the tread is suitable for mountain biking. Spring visitors will enjoy a diversity of wildflowers, including spiderwort and puccoon. Deer and wild turkey are present year-round. Be aware that the grassland is used for cattle grazing, and that ticks or poison ivy can be found along the trail.

The trailhead has a gravel parking area, an interpretive sign and map, and hitching rails for horses. The SNG's Jorgen's Hollow Campground is next door and there is a popular private horse camp only a mile further north on County Road 23. Jorgen's Hollow

ABOVE The North Country Trail in the Sheyenne National Grassland.

Campground has 14 primitive campsites, seven of these allow horses. There are two vault toilets and a hand pump for potable water. Occupancy is first come, first served. Camping is allowed anywhere on the grassland. Though water may be found in stock dams and Iron Springs Creek, any creek water should be treated before use.

From the parking area (at 28.4 miles per the NCT mileposts) the North Country Trail (NCT) swings east then south through a meadow that can be marshy in wet weather. It passes through a small grove of oak trees before crossing gravel County Road 23 at MP 28 and a pair of gates at 0.4 mile (N46 31.173, W97 12.045). The potentially wettest part of the trail is just across the road, but once the trail reaches the next grove of trees, the surface is reliably dry and shady as the trail stays mostly on the low hills covered by bur oak for the next two miles. Reach a gate at 1.6 miles (26.8 miles) where columbine can be found growing in the spring.

Reach a second gate at 1.9 miles (26.5 miles) before emerging into the open grassland at 2.4 miles (MP 26). Look for spring wildflowers here, including prairie smoke. At 2.9 miles (25.5 miles), there is a gate within sight of a windmill and two seasonal stock ponds. Reach the final gate on this section after traversing a brief shady area at 3.4 miles (MP 25). The trail next swings north to reach the wooden bridge over Iron Springs Creek, the only year-round flowing creek in the entire SNG, at 4.2 miles (24.2 miles and N31 30.642, W97 15.511).

On the west bank of the creek are a grove of trees and potential camp spots. In 2011, the bridge was damaged by undercutting on the west bank due to spring flooding, but it has since been repaired. This wooden bridge is 50 feet long and has a clear span of over 12 feet, hence the wooden guard rails on both sides of the bridge.

OAK LEAF TRAIL LOOP, SHEYENNE RANGER DISTRICT

A scenic loop hike based from the Jorgen's Hollow Campground.

GENERAL LOCATION: 19 miles north of Wyndmere, North Dakota.

HIGHLIGHT: An easy scenic loop that uses part of the North Country National Scenic Trail.

ACCESS: To access the east trailhead for the North Country Trail from the junction of State Highways 18 and 46 just south of the community of Leonard, drive south for five miles on paved County Road 23. Next turn left and drive east one mile on gravel County Road 2. Then turn right onto gravel County Road 23 and drive south four miles to the signed trailhead (N46 31.383, W97 12.175). Or, from the town of Lisbon, drive 22 miles east on ND 27 to the junction with gravel County Road 4. Turn left and drive north to a signed junction with County Road 23 at 26 miles. At 28.7 miles, reach the North Country trailhead on the right. The trailhead has a gravel parking area, signboard, and register box.

DISTANCE: This segment is a 4.2-mile loop. A 2.4-mile round trip extension is available for those would like to go to the end of the North Country Trail in the Sheyenne National Grassland.

ALLOWED USES: This trail is open to all non-motorized users, including hikers, mountain bikers, and horseback riders.

MAPS: Sheyenne National Grassland North Country and Oak Leaf Trails, USGS Coburn and Power, ND quadrangles, and Map E.

LEFT The North Country Trail leaving the Sheyenne National Grassland.
ABOVE The North Country Trail east of Jorgen's Hollow.

Completed in 2013, the Oak Leaf Trail is the newest trail on the Sheyenne National Grassland and is perhaps the most interesting trail for those who are not trying to complete the entire the North Country Trail. The 4.2-mile loop is based out of the new Jorgen's Hollow Campground, completed in 2015, and includes a nearly two mile long section of the NCT.

From the trailhead (N46 31.383, W97 12.175), take the short feeder trail straight ahead to intersect the North Country Trail and then turn left to follow the loop clockwise. The North Country Trail enters Jorgen's Hollow Campground at a gate. Exit the campground at 0.3 mile and traverse a pretty forest area dominated by oak. There is abundant poison ivy in the understory here, so it is best to stay on the trail. The wide trail is marked by a distinct tread with gravel surfacing and the tall wooden marker posts used by both the Maah Daah Hey and North Country Trails. At 0.8 mile, reach MP 29 (N46 31.540, W97 11.519) for the North Country Trail.

At 1.2 miles, cross a self-closing gate and enter a more open grassland. Cross an old two-track road at 1.4 miles. At 1.7 miles, reach the intersection with the Oak Leaf Trail (N46 31.597, W97 10.670). Here the North Country Trail turns left to reach the boundary of the Sheyenne National Grassland just past MP 31 (N46 31.771, W97 09.995) in 1.2 miles. The loop turns right and heads south on the Oak Leaf Trail.

ABOVE A welcome shady section of trail.

One plant on the grassland that travelers can't help but notice is leafy spurge. Leafy spurge is a widely established perennial weed infesting almost one million acres of land in North Dakota. Where thickly established, spurge can completely dominate the landscape, casting a pale yellow haze across the prairie. The plant is best known for its flower-like yellow-green bracts which appear in late May and early June, well before the actual small green flowers. Leafy spurge has a thick root system that can be 15 feet deep and produces seed pods that can distribute seeds up to 15 feet. It is one of the first plants to emerge in the spring and this early and rapid growth gives leafy spurge a competitive advantage over crop and pasture plants. The spread of leafy spurge has been reduced from a peak of 1.5 million acres by a control program started in the 1980s that includes several species of flea beetles.

The Oak Leaf Trail will criss-cross an old two-track road, then turn west in a small grove of trees at 2.4 miles. Pass a windmill and water tank on the left at 2.7 miles. At 3.0 miles, cross a gate and re-enter a mixed terrain of grasslands and trees. At 4.0 miles, reach an intersection where the North Country Trail enters from the left (N46 31.328, W97 12.040). MP 28 on the NCT is 0.2 mile left where the NCT crosses County Road 4.

Our loop turns right and follows the NCT to the end of the feeder trail and back to the trailhead parking. The Jorgen's Hollow Campground has 14 primitive sites, 7 sites are for horse parties, 7 are for campers without horses, some are well-shaded. Amenities include vault toilets and drinking water. Each site has a fire ring and picnic table. Camping is first come, first served.

ABOVE A boardwalk protects a damp section of the North Country Trail.

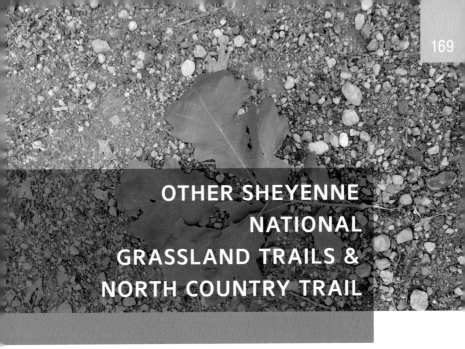

OTHER SHEYENNE NATIONAL GRASSLAND TRAILS & NORTH COUNTRY TRAIL

NORTH COUNTRY TRAIL, SHEYENNE NATIONAL GRASSLAND

The remaining sections of the North Country Trail (MP 6-24) in the Sheyenne National Grassland not covered in detail above can be easily hiked or ridden from the Middle trailhead. To reach the Middle trailhead from Lisbon, North Dakota, drive sixteen miles east on ND 27 to the junction with County Road 53 and turn left to drive 2.5 miles north to the Middle trailhead. The Middle trailhead is located just east of MP 15. A nine-mile, one-way trip to the west will take you to the end of the southwest section at MP 6 at the crossing of ND 27. This section crosses an active Canadian Pacific Railroad line and crosses some sand hills.

From Middle trailhead, another nine-mile, one-way trip to the east will take you to the Iron Creek Bridge and an additional four miles will bring you to the East trailhead by Jorgen's Hollow Campground.

HANKINSON HILLS TRAIL, SHEYENNE NATIONAL GRASSLAND

The Hankinson Hills are four square miles of wooded sand hills between the towns of Hankinson and Mantador in the extreme southeast corner of North Dakota. This outlying area of the Sheyenne National Grassland contains the 7.8-mile Hankinson Hills Trail. This

LEFT Oaks on the trail.
ABOVE Bur Oak is common in the Sheyenne National Grassland.

trail was built in 2004 for use by hikers, mountain bikers, and horseback riders. The trail has a compact gravel surface similar to that of the North Country Trail, is marked with sturdy wooden posts branded with an "HH" logo, and has mile markers.

Most use of the trail is by horse groups. ATVs are not allowed on the trail. The Hankinson Hills Campground was opened by the SNG in the summer of 2006 at the trailhead. There are separate loops for campers with (9 sites) and without (6 sites) horses. Potable water and vaulted toilets are available in both loops. There is a small fee for camping and a free picnic area.

To reach the trail and campground from I-29, take Exit 8 and head west to Hankinson, North Dakota on Highway 11. Continue west on Highway 11, go about two miles past Hankinson, and turn north onto 165th Avenue SE. Travel north for about 1.5 miles and turn west onto 91st Street SE. Travel west for about 1.25 miles and turn north into the Hankinson Hills unit. Continue north until you reach the campground. In addition to the campground, there are trailheads at the south and north end. Mile markers start at the north end.

FORT RANSOM STATE PARK SECTION, NORTH COUNTRY NATIONAL SCENIC TRAIL

A 3.0-mile section of the North Country Trail is located about 20 miles northwest of the Sheyenne National Grassland section in Fort Ransom State Park. This 890-acre park was opened in 1979 and has been substantially upgraded since then. The North Country Trail follows the west bank of the Sheyenne River across the length of the park. This trail segment is also open to mountain biking, horseback riding, cross-country skiing, and snowshoeing. There are at least 16 other trails in the park covering 20 miles, including one segment of the Sheyenne Valley Snowmobile Trail. Except for the 0.3-mile Riverside Trail, horses and mountain bikes are allowed on the trails in Fort Ransom. The park entry fee in 2019 was $7.

The park is located about two miles north of the town of Fort Ransom and on the Sheyenne River on the Walt Hjelle Parkway about three miles north on County Road 58. The easiest way to enjoy some of the North Country Trail is to park at the North Country trailhead behind the visitor center and follow the trail along the west bank of the Sheyenne River. At 1.2 miles, reach an intersection (N46 33.487, W97 55.344) with the Redetzke Ridge Trail. You can either return to the trailhead by the same route or continue on the combined North Country and Redetzke Ridge trails to complete a 4.0-mile loop.

LAKE SAKAKAWEA STATE PARK SECTION, NORTH COUNTRY NATIONAL SCENIC TRAIL

The western end of the North Country National Scenic Trail is found at Lake Sakakawea State Park, near Pick City and the Garrison Dam on the Missouri River. The final 1.8 miles of the North Country Trail lead from the park entry station south along the shore of Lake Sakakawea to ND 200 through short grass prairie and wooded coulees. In the park, the North Country Trail intersects the 2.7-mile Shoreline Trail, the 0.4-mile Overlook Trail, and the 0.2-mile Whitetail Trail. This section of the North Country Trail is open to hiking and mountain bikes.

The park is located two miles north of Pick City off ND 200 and is very popular with anglers and boaters on the 368,000-acre lake. There is a full-service marina, cabins, campgrounds, a store, and a swimming beach. There are also public campgrounds operated by the Army Corps of Engineers near Garrison Dam. The park is a fee area.

ABOVE Fall sunset at Fort Ransom State Park.

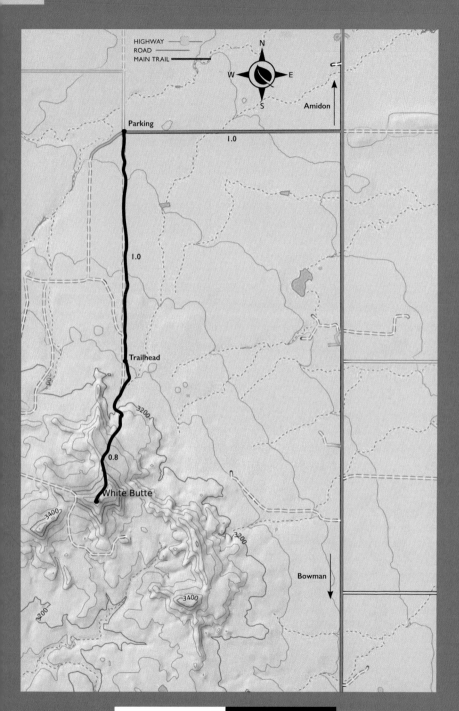

HIGHWAY
ROAD
MAIN TRAIL

N
W E
S

Amidon

Parking

1.0

1.0

Trailhead

3200

0.8

White Butte

3400

3200

3400

3200

Bowman

0.5   1.0 mi

5

OTHER NORTH DAKOTA AREAS
WHITE BUTTE ROUTE
PRIVATE LAND, THE HIGHEST POINT IN NORTH DAKOTA

An easy off-trail hike across private land to the highest point in North Dakota.

GENERAL LOCATION: Seven miles south of Amidon, North Dakota.

HIGHLIGHT: Surprising views and prairie scenery.

ACCESS: From Amidon, drive east 2.0 miles on US 85. Turn south at a sign for White Butte onto gravel 140th Ave SW (N46 28.949, W103 16.796). Drive 5.0 miles south on the well-maintained road and take a right turn on a gravel road (N46 24.607, W103 16.791). There currently are no signs for this road, but there is an overhead line on the right, or north side, of the road. Drive 1.0 mile west to the parking area where another dirt road joins from the right. There is a donation tube on the far right of the intersection and a parking sign opposite the intersection (N46 24.598, W103 18.029). White Butte is located directly to the south.

DISTANCE: The climb is 3.5 miles round trip.

ALLOWED USES: This route is open to day hikers only.

MAPS: USGS Amidon, ND, 7.5-minute quadrangle and Map F.

ABOVE Approaching White Butte from the north.

The highest point in North Dakota lies in the Chalky Buttes in the southwest part of the state. The buttes form a major divide between the Little Missouri River on the west and Cedar Creek and the Cannonball River, which drain east into the Missouri River. White Butte can be easily climbed in half a day, and it is close to US 85, the road that connects the Black Hills to Theodore Roosevelt National Park. The trip is especially popular with "highpointers," those who aspire to climb the high points of all fifty states.

White Butte is private property, owned by locals Daryle and Mary Dennis. In 2018, the landowners and the Highpointers Foundation signed a Trail Access Easement to provide permanent recreation access to the top of White Butte along the route from the north described here. The agreement gives the foundation the ability to build and maintain the trail to the summit. Trail users should consider leaving a donation in the tube at the trailhead. Note that the area has a reputation for rattlesnakes. Please also note that an older access point on the east side of White Butte is now closed.

From the parking area, walk south on a grassy old two-track road next to a fence line. Enjoy some extremely flat hiking across the grassland to reach an abandoned farm building on the right at 0.7 mile. At 1.0 mile, reach a gate and a sign for the White Butte trailhead (N46 23.738, W103 18.034). Continue south along the fence line to the edge of the grassland on the north face of the butte facing into a badlands draw. There is a well-defined path up the left side of the draw that may be marked with small cairns. Near the top of the draw, you'll briefly rejoin the fence line before setting off across the grassland toward the north facing ridge of White Butte. Crest the ridge at a small saddle and follow the ridgeline north to reach the well-marked summit at 1.75 miles (N46 23.244, W103 18.154). To complete the hike, return to the parking area by retracing your route.

The 3,506 foot-high summit has a USGS Survey marker, a register box, large summit cairn, and a memorial marker for Laurence Buzalsky, a former owner of the property who died in 1990. The USGS marker placed in 1962 illustrates the speed of erosion in the badlands climate. At the time of my first visit in 1988, the top 12 inches were exposed, and by 2019 nearly 32 inches were exposed.

The Chalky Buttes are an exceptionally pretty area. To the south of White Butte at the head of Sand Creek are badlands that equal some of those found in Theodore Roosevelt National Park, or the Sage Creek Wilderness in South Dakota's Badlands National Park. To the north and west, across US 85 are the Dakota Prairie Grasslands and the Black Buttes.

White Butte lies on the southwest side of the Williston Basin, a major oil-producing region. In the center of the Williston Basin, the bedrock is mostly Paleocene-age Sentinel Butte Formation. The Chalky Buttes are a relict island of younger Oligocene-age White River Group sedimentary rocks standing above the prairie. The tops of White Butte, Radio Tower Butte, and Black Butte are capped by even younger Tertiary sedimentary rocks.

For many years, a sign on US 85 caused confusion about the location of White Butte. The sign seemed to point to a butte and radio tower only a mile east of the highway. At 3,472 feet, the Radio Tower Butte is still one of the highest points in the state, but not the highest. The sign was moved to a point east of Amidon so that it now points to the correct butte. This confusion has caused several "highpointers," and a few North Dakota natives, to return to the Chalky Buttes to reach the correct summit.

ABOVE An abandoned farm building along the approach to White Butte.

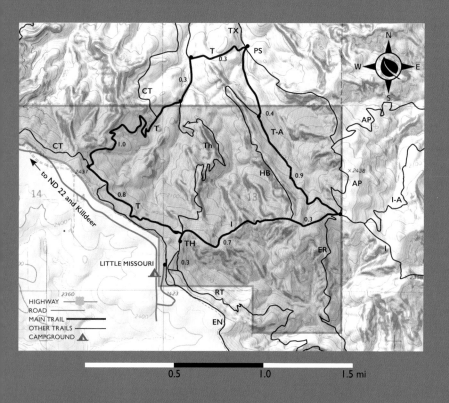

LITTLE MISSOURI

to ND 22 and Killdeer

HIGHWAY
ROAD
MAIN TRAIL
OTHER TRAILS
CAMPGROUND

0.5   1.0   1.5 mi

N
W   E
S

INDIAN-TRAVOIS TRAILS LOOP, LITTLE MISSOURI STATE PARK

A journey from the prairie through the badlands to the Little Missouri River for horses and hikers.

GENERAL LOCATION: Twenty-one miles northeast of Killdeer, North Dakota.

HIGHLIGHT: Little-used horse trails in a natural setting.

ACCESS: From Killdeer, drive 18 miles north on North Dakota Highway 22. Turn east onto the signed gravel park road and drive 2.3 miles to the day use parking area, which is located across from the ranger station (N47 32.817, W102 44.149).

DISTANCE: The loop is 5.3 miles around.

ALLOWED USES: Park trails are open to hikers and horseback riders only. Mountain biking is prohibited.

MAPS: Little Missouri State Park Trail Map, USGS Mandaree SW, ND 7.5-minute quadrangle; and Map G.

Little Missouri State Park is a hidden gem for horseback riders and hikers seeking to explore the North Dakota badlands. A large network of 20 trails covering 48 miles is concealed in a small state park. The park is maintained for visitors seeking camping and horseback and hiking trails and is open seasonally from May to October. The park charges a small entry fee ($7 in 2019). Horseback riders will also need to purchase a horse pass (currently $6/day/horse). A loop combining the Indian and

ABOVE Badlands above the Little Missouri River.

Travois trails is the quickest route to descend from the grassland bluffs to the Little Missouri River bottomlands 500 feet below.

The park trails are marked by carsonite posts labelled with the letter abbreviation for the trail: "I" for Indian, "T" for Travois, etc. In 2006, the park received a $25,000 Recreation Trails Grant from the Federal Highway Administration to improve and add trails at Little Missouri and the trails have since been upgraded. Trails are marked as easiest (green), intermediate (blue), or most difficult (black) based on the perspective of horseback riders. Hikers and horseback riders are restricted to designated trails.

From the day use parking area near the ranger station (N47 132.817, W102 44.149), follow the campground road to the north past one set of corrals and bear right at the start of a second corral loop on the left. The road will descend past a final campsite and corral to reach the main trailhead at 0.3 mile (N47 32.999, W102 44.059).

Three trails leave from the trailhead at a well-signed gate. Your return route on the Travois (T) Trail enters on the left, while Thors (TH) Trail starts straight ahead. Your outbound route is the Indian (I) Trail which leads right and descends from the bluffs through a grove of junipers, then enters badlands. At 0.6 mile, reach a junction with a spur of the Thors Trail on the left that does not appear on the park map. Climb up and over a small ridge, then stay right at the junction with the Hogback (HB) Trail at 1.0 mile.

At 1.3 miles, reach the start of a complicated 5-way intersection. Ignore the Eagle Rock (ER) Trail that splits off to the right, and then take the Travois (T) Trail which splits left at a signpost that is just off the crest of the ridge. If you overshoot the Travois Trail, you will immediately come to another fork where the Aspen Pass (AP) Trail goes left and the Indian (I) Trail continues to the right (N47 33.078, W102 42.941).

At the 5-way, turn left and north onto the Travois (T) Trail and descend steadily toward the Little Missouri River. The descent begins steeply through juniper and some grasslands, then becomes more gradual. Watch carefully for thin black lignite seams and thick bands of gray bentonite clay. Intersect the upper end of the Hogback (HB) Trail at 2.2 miles (N47 33.541, W102 43.477). Just beyond this intersection, cross through a gate with a map board. This gate marks the limit of state-owned land and you are now entering private lands that have been leased by the park.

At 2.6 miles (N47 33.861, W102 43.639), reach another key intersection by a stock tank where you are likely to encounter cattle. Here the Petrified Stump (PS) Trail turns sharply right up an old two-track road to climb back toward the Aspen Pass Trail. The TX (TX) Trail continues straight ahead toward the Little Missouri River bottomlands. Though the park and other topo maps show that the river is close by, the channel has since migrated to the north and is not easily accessed by the TX Trail. Our route is not well-marked here, but follows the Travois Trail to the left and southwest up a small draw on an old two-track road.

At 2.9 miles, continue to the left at a signed trail post where the Cedar Top (CT) Trail goes right. At 3.2 miles (N47 33.607, W102 44.077), reach another gate and map board that marks your return to the state-owned property. Here, Thors (TH) Trail splits left while the loop continues right on the Travois Trail. The Cedar Top (CT) Trail will enter again on the right before the Travois Trail makes an obscure turn to the right just past an abandoned stock tank. The tank marks the start of the climb back to the upper grasslands, but the climb offers some great badlands scenery as compensation for the effort expended in the climb.

At 4.2 miles, the trail entering on the right by a small pond is marked as the Shady Lane (SL) Trail, but is actually the upper end of the Cedar Top Trail (N47 33.382, W102 44.710). Just beyond, cross an old two-track road and then reach a sign for Hannah's Pass that explains that the trail was rebuilt using funds donated in memory of Hannah Kramer. At 4.5 miles, Shady Lane Trail joins on the right. Close the loop at the intersections with the I and TH trails at the prominent gate at the end of the campground road at 5.0 miles. Follow the campground road south to return to the day use parking area at 5.3 miles.

Little Missouri State Park has excellent camping facilities. There are 3 primitive campsites, 28 with electricity and 5 of these have rental shelters available. The park campground has vault toilets and pay showers. There are 81 horse corrals and artesian wells for horses. A horse-riding concession, horse rentals, and guide service are available in season. Campsites can be booked 95 days in advance and can be made online or by phone (800-807-4723).

Besides the solitude of a primitive park, visitors come for the wildlife watching. Coyotes, mule deer, eagles, badgers, and prairie dogs are found along with prairie rattlesnakes. The park is located along the final free-flowing stretch of the Little Missouri before its waters become impounded as part of Lake Sakakawea behind Garrison Dam on the Missouri River.

The park feels much bigger than it really is. In addition to the 4,500 acres of park land, the state leases river bottomland, which is controlled by the Army Corps of Engineers, and other land from private owners. Since the land is leased for riding only, there is no grazing of horses allowed. Visitors are asked not to disturb cattle and should avoid riding through areas where cattle are grazing. The park also discourages riding when trails are wet, both to avoid hazardous conditions and to maintain the trails in good riding and hiking conditions.

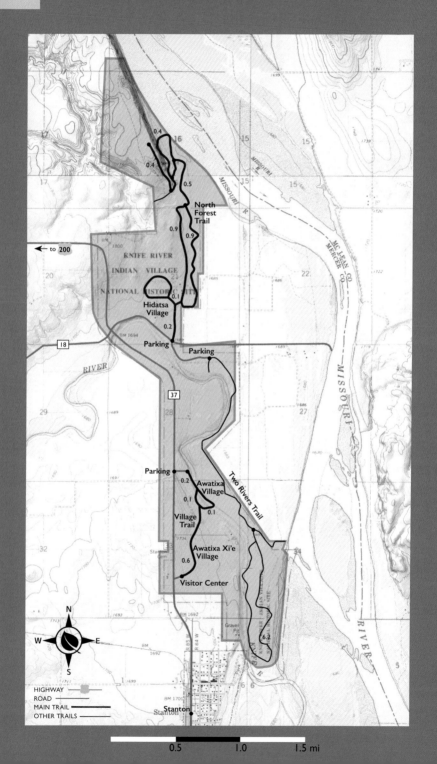

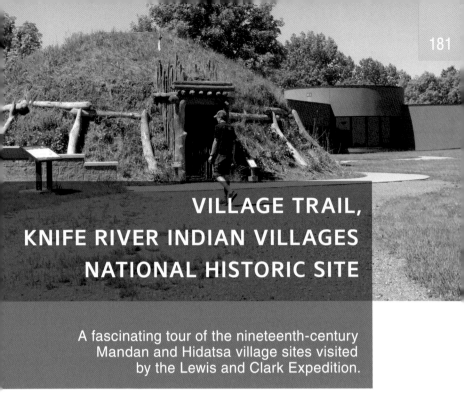

VILLAGE TRAIL, KNIFE RIVER INDIAN VILLAGES NATIONAL HISTORIC SITE

A fascinating tour of the nineteenth-century Mandan and Hidatsa village sites visited by the Lewis and Clark Expedition.

GENERAL LOCATION: One mile north of Stanton, North Dakota.

HIGHLIGHT: The Earthlodge and the Sakakawea and Lower Hidatsa village sites.

ACCESS: From Bismarck, drive 36 miles north on US 83 to Washburn. Turn left onto ND 200A and drive 20 miles west to the junction with ND 31. Turn right and drive 2.5 miles north through the town of Stanton to reach the entry to the park visitor center (N47 19.896, W101 23.165). From the west, Take Exit 127 off Interstate 94 and drive 30 miles north. Turn right onto the combined ND 31 and 200A for 1.8 miles. Then turn left and drive 2.5 miles north through the town of Stanton to reach the entry to the park visitor center.

DISTANCE: The hike out and back to the Awatixa Village is 1.7 miles round trip.

ALLOWED USES: This trail is open to day hikers only.

MAPS: NPS Knife River Indian Villages National Historic Site, USGS Stanton, ND 7.5-minute quadrangle, and Map H.

ABOVE The Earth Lodge at Knife River.

The Knife River Indian Villages National Historic Site does a tremendous job of interpreting the centuries-old villages at the mouth of the Knife River. Any first-time visitors should allot time in the visitor center to explore the park museum, learn about the history and culture of the Hidatsa people, and to view the short film about the life of Buffalo Bird Woman who lived at the villages. To gain a better understanding of how the villagers lived, you can also ask at the front desk for a guided tour of the park's reconstructed Earthlodge.

Traditional earthlodge construction began with the setting of four corner posts to form a central core. Next came an outer circle of posts and cross beams, and rafters placed above the central core. Split logs were laid along the outer posts to form a wall, then bunches of willow branches, dried prairie grass, and thick sod formed the outer shell. There was a central fireplace and a smoke hole that could be covered. Food was stored in a pit accessible by ladder from inside the lodge. Earthlodges typically were 30 to 60 feet across and lasted about ten years. Each earthlodge held an extended family. Families typically moved in winter to other lodges located on the river bottomlands where wood for fires was more easily available. The 40-foot diameter Knife River Earthlodge was built in 1995 by the National Park Service using traditional materials.

The gravel Village Trail begins at the back side of the visitor center. The trail passes the Earthlodge and a Hidatsa garden growing the beans, squash, and corn that were the tribe's dietary staples. The trail then turns north to reach the Awatixa Xi'e (Lower Hidatsa) Village site at 0.25 mile. Little remains here 200 years after the peak occupation of these sites, but 51 shallow circular depressions still mark the sites of individual lodges, packed together along the riverbank.

The slow erosion of the village sites by the Knife River is more apparent at Awatixa (Sakakawea) Village at 0.7 mile (N47 20.343, W101 22.949). Here, many of the original 52 lodge sites have been destroyed by river erosion or by modern farming. It was most likely at this village in 1804 that Lewis and Clark first met Toussaint Charbonneau and his wife Sakakawea and hired them to join the expedition as interpreters.

Despite the construction of protective berms along the river, bank erosion is still active. In the spring of 2019, the Knife River side of the loop around the Awatixa Village site and the spur trail to the parking area on the north end both were closed due to erosion caused by heavy spring runoff. The loop around the Awatixa Village was closed at the stairs that lead down to a short section of trail along the river's edge. After exploring the Awatixa Village retrace your steps back to the visitor center.

LEFT Phlox blooming along the North Forest Trail at Knife River.

The Mandan and Hidatsa tribes lived along the Upper Missouri River for several hundred years before their first contact with white explorers. Three subtribes of the Hidatsa—the Awatixa, the Awaxawi, and the Hidatsa-Proper—settled into prosperous villages near the confluence of the Knife and Missouri Rivers. They established permanent earthlodge villages and raised several crops, including corn, beans, squash, and sunflowers. Sakakawea was living in the villages in the winter of 1804-1805 with her French-Canadian husband when they were hired to be guides and interpreters by the expedition of Lewis and Clark.

The location of the Mandan and Hidatsa on the Missouri allowed the tribes to function as middlemen for the flourishing trade between other tribes. But further contact with whites and the arrival of fur traders changed the economy of the northern plains. The tribes became more dependent on manufactured goods, and as with so many other tribes, new diseases decimated their population. Along with the Arrikaras, the Mandan and Hidatsa were moved upstream to the Fort Berthold Reservation in 1885.

Knife River Indian Villages is located on the Missouri River at the confluence with the Knife River. The 1,578-acre park was established in 1974. The visitor center and Earthlodge are open 9 A.M. to 9 P.M. central time in summer and 8:30 to 4:30 in winter, and are closed Thanksgiving, Christmas, and New Year's Day. Park trails and grounds are open daily from sunrise until sunset. There is no picnic area, campground, or entrance fee.

ABOVE The Knife River in spring.
RIGHT Hidatsa Village on the North Forest Trail.

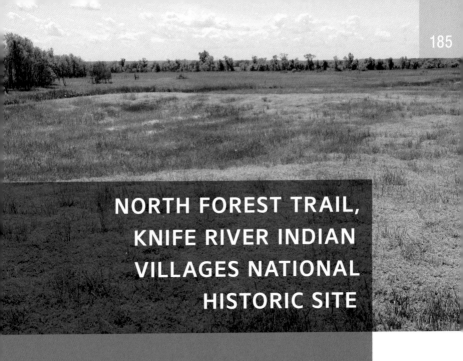

NORTH FOREST TRAIL, KNIFE RIVER INDIAN VILLAGES NATIONAL HISTORIC SITE

A partly-forested walk to an overlook above the Knife River.

GENERAL LOCATION: Three miles north of Stanton, North Dakota.

HIGHLIGHT: A stop at Hidatsa Village.

ACCESS: From Bismarck, drive 36 miles north on US 83 to Washburn. Turn left onto ND 200A and drive 20 miles west to the junction with ND 31. Turn right and drive 4.6 miles north through the town of Stanton, past the park visitor center, and over the bridge above the Knife River. Turn right immediately after the bridge and follow the gravel County Road 18 (4th Street SW) for 0.6 mile to the signed trailhead (N47 21.444, W101 23.194). From the west, take Exit 127 off Interstate 94 and drive 30 miles north. Turn right onto the combined ND 31 and 200A for 1.8 miles. Then turn left and drive 4.6 miles north through the town of Stanton, past the park visitor center, and over the bridge above the Knife River. Turn right immediately after the bridge and follow the gravel County Road 18 (4th Street SW) for 0.6 mile to the signed trailhead.

DISTANCE: The hike to the end of the overlook is 2.7 miles one way. By skipping the side trips and cutting short the upper loop, the return trip can be made in 2.2 miles for a roundtrip of 4.9 miles. If you just plan to visit Hidatsa Village, the roundtrip walk is 0.6 mile.

ALLOWED USES: This trail is open to day hikers only.

MAPS: NPS Knife River Indian Villages National Historic Site, USGS Stanton and Garrison Dam South, ND 7.5-minute quadrangles, and Map H.

The North Forest Trail offers visitors a different view of the Historic Site than does the more popular Village Trail. North Forest explores a long belt of green ash, box elder, willow, and some cottonwood trees along the floodplain of the Missouri River, visits a scenic overlook, and still manages to take in an important settlement site at Hidatsa Village.

The configuration of the North Forest Trail is a bit complicated. The trail has a long southern loop and a smaller loop at the north end. There is a connector trail from the trailhead to the southern loop and another connector between the two loops. A side trail leads to Hidatsa Village from the start of the southern loop and side trails lead from the end of the northern loop to an overlook above the river and to another trailhead.

From the North Forest trailhead, walk north along a mowed path with a fence line to your right. At 0.2 mile, turn left at a sign for the side trip to Hidatsa Village (N47 21.688, W101 23.284), also known as the Big Hidatsa Site. Reach an interpretive panel at the edge of the site at 0.3 mile. Hidatsa people lived at this site from about 1600 to 1845, building as many as 113 earthlodges which sheltered up to 800 to 1200 people. As is the case along the Village Trail, all that remain on the surface of the site are the circular depressions that mark the individual lodge locations. The site was abandoned in 1845 when the Hidatsa moved upriver to Like-a-Fishhook Village, to be joined by the Mandan and Arikaras, in the aftermath of the smallpox epidemic of the late 1830s. Like-a-Fishhook proved to be the tribe's last traditional earthlodge village. In the late 1880s, the village was abandoned and all three tribes were forced to move to the then Fort Berthold Indian Reservation. Like-a-Fishhook Village is now covered by the waters of Lake Sakakawea, which are backed up by Garrison Dam on the Missouri River.

Return to the main trail at 0.4 mile and go left to hike the mowed southern loop clockwise. This forested stretch of trail passes through a rich understory of thick grass and carpets of purple phlox. Unfortunately, the tree canopy here has been devastated by disease.

Much of the park's forest has a fungus disease killing all the mature green ash trees and many of the younger saplings. The disease is readily visible by its conk mushrooms along the outer bark of the tree. The visible conks are like the tip of an iceberg, with most of the damage lying below the bark layer. The park is in the process of removing the infected trees and allowing for the succession of younger disease-resistant trees to replace the dead and dying ones. The forest is also plagued by inch worms which are feeding in the damaged canopy. Their sticky hanging webs can be a major nuisance to hikers.

At 1.3 miles, reach the end of the loop (N47 22.294, W101 23.116) and turn left on a connector trail to continue north along the edge of the woods. At 1.8 miles, reach the northern loop (N47 22.595, W101 23.133) by a bench and river view and go right to walk the loop counterclockwise. At 2.2 miles, reach a trail junction at the end of the northern loop. Go straight to reach a split where the North Prairie Arm goes right for 0.4 mile and a short spur leads left to an alternate trailhead. The mowed North Prairie Arm leads to the highest point in the park, views of the Missouri River, and the finest stand of native prairie in the park (N47 22.692, W101 23.477). This is a remnant of original prairie that has never been plowed.

From the overlook, the easiest way back to the main trailhead is to retrace your route to the northern loop, bear right on the short side of the loop, and follow the main connector back to the southern loop. Walk the river side of the south loop, then take the feeder trail to the trailhead.

Conditions permitting, the North Forest Trail is open for snowshoeing and cross-country skiing in winter. The trail is more sheltered from wind and sun than Two Rivers, and it may offer skiers more reliable snow.

Knife River's Two Rivers Trail also begins from a parking area off County Road 18. The trail follows an old two-track road and begins in a narrow strip of grassland between the Knife River and cultivated land outside the park. A loop at the south end of the trail passes through a riverside forest of green ash, willow, box elder, and cottonwoods and offers views of both the Knife and Missouri Rivers. This trail is 6.2-miles long and is groomed for cross-country skiing in winter when conditions permit.

ABOVE The start of the North Forest Trail at Knife River.

OTHER TRAILS

CROSS RANCH STATE PARK AND NATURE PRESERVE

Cross Ranch State Park preserves seven miles of one of the last free-flowing and undeveloped stretches of the Missouri River. The narrow 590-acre park is one of the few opportunities on the northern Great Plains to hike in a wooded landscape. In addition to the trail system, the park features a visitor center, boat launch area, canoe and kayak rentals, cabins, tipis, and yurts for rent, as well as both tent and RV campgrounds. The park is adjacent to the Nature Conservancy's 5,000-acre Cross Ranch Preserve. The park is located just 26 miles south of the Knife River Indian Villages National Historic Site. There are 16 miles of trail in the park and adjacent preserve.

The main park trail system is essentially a string of six main loops plus some long skinny loops along the riverside in the southern end of the park. At the north end of the park, the Levis Trail (2.2 miles) contains a single backcountry campsite with a vault toilet. The Gaines (2.1 miles) and Cottonwood (3.3 miles) Trails are located on land owned by the Nature Conservancy's Cross Ranch Nature Preserve and follow a jeep track still used by researchers. The Matah Trail (2.4 miles) starts at the visitor center and forms a series of three smaller loops through the park's central developed area. The innermost loop follows a self-guiding interpretive route for which brochures are available at the visitor center.

The upper (2.5 miles) and lower (1.7 miles) loops of the Ma-ak-oti Trail begin from the Sanger trailhead in the southern part of the park and connect to the Matah Trail. There are steep unprotected stairs on these trails. The Ma-ak-oti Trail is open for snowshoeing in winter, while the other park trails are open to cross-country skiing. In 2004, the entire trail system was included in the National Recreation Trail System.

Adjacent to Cross Ranch State Park is the 6,000-acre Cross Ranch Nature Preserve, owned and operated by the Nature Conservancy, which is a private, nonprofit organization devoted to the preservation of ecologically sensitive lands and the habitats of threatened plants and animals. The ranch consists of three units covering 5,600 acres. The 1,800-acre north unit is on the banks of the Missouri and borders the state park. The other two units are on the hills above the river floodplain. There are no public facilities at ranch headquarters. The Nature Conservancy keeps bison on the central and south units of the ranch. The self-guided Prairie Trail (2.0 miles) crosses prairie, wooded draws, and bison pasture. Brochures can be found at the trailhead, located 0.75 mile north of the park entrance on the gravel road. The Prairie Trail is not open for skiing.

FORT UNION TRADING POST NATIONAL HISTORIC SITE

The Fort Union Trading Post National Historic Site was established in 1966 near the confluence of the Missouri and Yellowstone Rivers. The original fort was established in 1829 by the American Fur Company as a trading post with the Assiniboine, Crow, and Blackfoot Indian tribes. Trade relations gradually deteriorated, and the fort was sold to the U.S. Army and dismantled in 1867. Since the National Park Service acquired the property in 1966, it has been excavating, reconstructing, and developing exhibits. Fort Union is located 24 miles southwest of Williston on ND 1804 close to the North Dakota-Montana border. The park is open daily except for New Year's Day and Christmas. The park has recently opened the one-mile roundtrip Bodmer Overlook Trail north of the fort across the railroad tracks. This trail leads to the location where famed artist Karl Bodmer once stood and painted the Assiniboine at Fort Union in the 1830s.

ABOVE Phlox is commonly found in the open woodlands at Knife River.

APPENDIX A - SELECTED BIBLIOGRAPHY

Fenn, Elizabeth A. *Encounters at the Heart of the World: A History of the Mandan People.* New York: Farrar, Straus and Giroux, 2015.

Froiland, Sven G. *Natural History of the Black Hills and Badlands.* Sioux Falls: The Center for Western Studies, 2016.

Hauk, Joy Keve. *Badlands: Its Life and Landscape.* Interior, South Dakota: Badlands Natural History Association, 1969.

Johnson, James R. and Gary E. Larson. *Grassland Plants of South Dakota and the Northern Great Plains.* Brookings: South Dakota State University Extension, 2016.

McCullough, David. *Mornings on Horseback: The Story of an Extraordinary Family, a Vanished Way of Life and the Unique Child Who Became Theodore Roosevelt.* New York: Simon and Schuster, 1982.

Morris, Edmund. *Theodore Rex.* New York: Modern Library, 2002.

Murphy, E. C., J. P. Bluemle, and B. M. Kaye. "A Road Log Guide for the South and North Units Theodore Roosevelt National Park." Medora, North Dakota: Theodore Roosevelt Nature and History Association, 2005.

National Geographic Trails Illustrated. "Theodore Roosevelt National Park Map (#259)."

Raventon, Edward. *Island in the Plains.* Denver: Johnson Books, 1994.

Raventon, Edward. *Buffalo Country: A Northern Plains Narrative.* Denver: Johnson Books, 2003.

Rogers, Hiram. *Exploring the Black Hills and Badlands: A Guide for Hikers, Cross-country Skiers, and Mountain Bikers.* Denver: Johnson Books, 1999.

Roosevelt, Theodore. *Ranch Life and the Hunting Trail.* New York: St. Martin's Press, 1985.

Schoch, Henry A. and Bruce M. Kaye. *Theodore Roosevelt: The Story Behind the Scenery.* Whittier, California: K.C. Publications, 1993.

Van Bruggen, Theodore. *Wildflowers, Grasses, and Other Plants of the Northern Plains and Black Hills.* Interior, South Dakota: Badlands Natural History Association, 1992.

Wefald, Susan. *Spectacular North Dakota Hikes: Bring the Dog.* Fargo: North Dakota State University Press, 2011.

APPENDIX B - INFORMATION SOURCES

Cross Ranch Nature Preserve, The Nature Conservancy, 1401 River Road, Center, ND 58530-9445, https://www.nature.org/en-us/get involved/how-to-help/places-we-protect/cross-ranch-preserve

Cross Ranch State Park, 1403 River Road, Center, ND 58530, (701) 794-3731, crsp@state.nd.us, www.parkrec.nd.gov/cross-ranch-state-park

Dakota Cyclery, 365 Main Street, PO Box 361, Medora, ND 58645, (701) 623-4808 or (888) 321-1218, www.dakotacyclery.com

Dakota Prairie Grasslands, 2000 Miriam Circle, Bismarck, ND 58501, (701) 989-7300, www.fs.usda.gov/main/dpg/home

Fort Abraham Lincoln State Park, 4480 Fort Lincoln Road, Mandan, ND 58554, (701) 667-6340. falsp@state.nd.us, www.parkrec.nd.gov/fort-abraham-lincoln-state-park

Fort Union Trading Post National Historic Site, 15550 Highway 1804, Williston, ND 58801, (701) 572-9083, www.nps.gov/fous

Grand River Ranger District, 1005 5th Avenue W, Lemmon, SD 57638, (605) 374-3592

Knife River Indian Villages National Historic Site, PO Box 9, Stanton, ND 58571, (701) 745-3300, www.nps.gov/knri

Lake Sakakawea State Park, 720 Park Avenue, Pick City, ND 58545, (701) 487-3315, lssp@nd.gov, www.parkrec.nd.gov/lake-sakakawea-state-park

Leave No Trace Center for Outdoor Ethics, PO Box 997, Boulder, CO 80306, (800) 332-4100, www.lnt.org

Lewis and Clark State Park, 4904 119th Road NW, Epping, ND 58843, (701) 859-3071, lcsp@state.nd.us, www.parkrec.nd.gov/lewis-clark-state-park

Little Missouri State Park, 910 103rd Avenue NW, Killdeer, ND 58640, (701) 764-5256, lmosp@nd.gov, www.parkrec.nd.gov/little-missouri-state-park-0

Maah Daah Hey Trail Association, PO Box 156, Bismarck, ND 58502, mdhta.com

McKenzie Ranger District, 1905 South Main Street, Watford City, ND 58854, (701) 842-8500

Medora Ranger District, 99 23rd Avenue W, Suite B, Dickinson, ND 58601, (701) 227-7800

North Dakota Badlands Horse, www.ndbh.org

National Geographic Trails Illustrated Maps, PO Box 4357, Evergreen, Colorado 80437-4357, (800) 962-1643, www.natgeomaps.com/trail-maps/trails-illustrated-maps

North Country National Scenic Trail, PO Box 288, Lowell, MI 49331, (616) 319-7906, www.nps.gov/noco

North Country Trail Association, 229 E. Main Street, Lowell, MI 49331, 866-HIKE-NCT, www.northcountrytrail.org

North Dakota State Parks and Recreation Department, 1600 E. Century Avenue, Suite 3, PO Box 5594, Bismarck, ND 58506, (701) 328-5357, parkrec@nd.gov, www.parkrec.nd.gov

North Dakota Tourism Division, Century Center, 1600 E. Century Avenue, Suite 2, PO Box 2057, Bismarck, ND 58503-2057, (800) 435-5663 or (701) 328-2525, www.ndtourism.com

Shadehill Recreation Area, 19150 Summerville Road, Shadehill, SD 57638, (605)374.5114, shadehill@state.sd.us, https://gfp.sd.gov/parks/detail/shadehill-recreation-area

Sheyenne Ranger District, 1601 Main Street, Lisbon, ND 58054, (701) 683-4342

Sully Creek State Park, 1465 36th Street, Medora ND, 58645, (701) 623-2024, scsp@nd.gov, www.parkrec.nd.gov/sully-creek-state-park

Theodore Roosevelt National Park, PO Box 7, Medora, ND 58645, (701) 623-4466 (South Unit), www.nps.gov/thro. The North Unit can be reached at (701) 842-2333.

Theodore Roosevelt Nature and History Association, 201 E. River Road N, PO Box 167, Medora, ND 58645, (701) 623-4884, info@trnha.org, www.trnha.org

ADDITIONAL SERVICES IN MEDORA

Billings County Sheriff, 495 4th Street, Medora, ND 58645, (701) 623-4323

Medora Convention and Visitors Bureau, PO Box 433, Medora, ND 58645, (701) 623-4830, www.medorand.com

Medora Police Department, 465 Pacific Avenue, Medora, ND 58645, (701) 623-4333

CHI St. Alexius Health Dickinson Medical Center, 2500 Fairway Street, Dickinson, ND 58601, (701) 456-4000

ADDITIONAL SERVICES IN WATFORD CITY

McKenzie County Healthcare Systems, Inc., 09 4th Avenue NE, Watford City, ND 58854, (701) 842-3000

McKenzie County Sheriff's Office, 1201 12th Street SE, Watford City, ND 58854, (701) 444-3654

Watford City Police Department, 1201 12th Street SE A, Watford City, ND 58854, (701) 842-2280

Visit Watford City, 100 2nd Avenue SW, Watford City, ND 5 8854-0699, 800-701-2804, www.visitwatfordcity.com

ABOVE Bison herd crossing the Little Missouri.

HIRAM ROGERS is the author of the bestselling *Exploring the Black Hills and Badlands*, as well as the books *50 Hikes in Kentucky* and *Backroad Bicycling in the Blue Ridge and Smoky Mountains*. He has also written about the outdoor recreation and conservation issues for several magazines, including *Backpacker* and *GORP.com*. He is a geologist; avid hiker, trail runner, and mountain biker; and former resident of the Dakotas.

Notes

Notes